Greater Than a Tour: Reviews from

I think the series is wonderful and beneficial for tourists to get information before visiting the city.

-Seckin Zumbul, Izmir Turkey

I am a world traveler who has read many trip guides but this one really made a difference for me. I would call it a heartfelt creation of a local guide expert instead of just a guide.

-Susy, Isla Holbox, Mexico

New to the area like me, this is a must have!

 -Joe, Bloomington, USA

This is a good series that gets down to it when looking for things to do at your destination without having to read a novel for just a few ideas.

-Rachel, Monterey, USA

Good information to have to plan my trip to this destination.

-Pennie Farrell, Mexico

Great ideas for a port day.

-Mary Martin USA

Aptly titled, you won't just be a tourist after reading this book. You'll be greater than a tourist!

-Alan Warner, Grand Rapids, USA

Even though I only have three days to spend in San Miguel in an upcoming visit, I will use the author's suggestions to guide some of my time there. An easy read - with chapters named to guide me in directions I want to go.

 -Robert Catapano, USA

Great insights from a local perspective! Useful information and a very good value!

-Sarah, USA

This series provides an in-depth experience through the eyes of a local. Reading these series will help you to travel the city in with confidence and it'll make your journey a unique one.

-Andrew Teoh, Ipoh, Malaysia

>TOURIST

GREATER THAN A TOURIST-SOUTH AFRICA

300 Travel Tips from Locals

Greater Than a Tourist-South Africa   Copyright © 2019 by CZYK Publishing LLC. All Rights Reserved.

All rights reserved. No part of this book may be reproduced in any form or by any electronic or mechanical means including information storage and retrieval systems, without permission in writing from the author. The only exception is by a reviewer, who may quote short excerpts in a review.

The statements in this book are of the authors and may not be the views of CZYK Publishing or Greater Than a Tourist.

Cover Image: https://pixabay.com/photos/elephant-herd-of-elephants-279505/

CZYK Publishing Since 2011.

Greater Than a Tourist
Visit our website at www.GreaterThanaTourist.com

Lock Haven, PA
All rights reserved.
ISBN: 9798656697743

>TOURIST

>TOURIST
50 TRAVEL TIPS FROM A LOCAL

>TOURIST

Greater Than a Tourist –Cape Town South Africa

Mia Masson

Greater Than a Tourist – Durban KwaZulu-Natal South Africa

Nazeera Rawat

GREATER THAN A TOURIST –JOHANNESBURG GAUTENG SOUTH AFRICA

Micheline Logan

GREATER THAN A TOURIST – PRETORIA GAUTENG SOUTH AFRICA

Natasha van der Schyff

GREATER THAN A TOURIST- PORT ELIZABETH SOUTH AFRICA

NELSON MANDELA BAY

Michel du Preez

Greater Than a Tourist –Sunshine Coast Route Eastern Cape Province South Africa

Kim Irvine

BOOK DESCRIPTION

Are you excited about planning your next trip?

Do you want to try something new?

Would you like some guidance from a local?

If you answered yes to any of these questions, then this Greater Than a Tourist book is for you.

Greater Than a Tourist- South Africa: 300 Travel Tips from Locals gives you the inside scoop on South Africa. Most travel books tell you how to travel like a tourist. Although there is nothing wrong with that, as part of the Greater Than a Tourist series, this book will give you travel tips from someone who has lived at your next travel destination.

In these pages, you will discover advice that will help you throughout your stay. This book will not tell you exact addresses or store hours but instead will give you excitement and knowledge from a local that you may not find in other smaller print travel books.

Travel like a local. Slow down, stay in one place, and get to know the people and the culture. By the time you finish this book, you will be eager and prepared to travel to your next destination.

Inside this travel guide book you will find:

- Insider tips from a local.

- A bonus book "50 Things to Know About Packing Light for Travel" by bestselling author *Manidipa Bhattacharyya*.

- A packing and planning list.

- A list of travel questions to ask yourself or others while traveling.

OUR STORY

Traveling is a passion of the "Greater than a Tourist" series creator. Lisa studied abroad in college, and for their honeymoon Lisa and her husband toured Europe. During her travels to Malta, an older man tried to give her some advice based on his own experience living on the island since he was a young boy. She was not sure if she should talk to the stranger but was interested in his advice. When traveling to some places she was wary to talk to locals because she was afraid that they weren't being genuine. Through her travels, Lisa learned how much locals had to share with tourists. Lisa created the "Greater Than a Tourist" book series to help connect people with locals. A topic that locals are very passionate about sharing.

>TOURIST

HOW TO USE THIS BOOK

The Greater Than a Tourist book series was written by someone who has lived in an area for over three months. The goal of this book is to help travelers either dream or experience different locations by providing opinions from a local. The author has made suggestions based on their own experiences. Please do your own research before traveling to the area in case the suggested places are unavailable.

Travel Advisories: As a first step in planning any trip abroad, check the Travel Advisories for your intended destination.
https://travel.state.gov/content/travel/en/traveladvisories/traveladvisories.html

\>TOURIST

FROM THE PUBLISHER

Traveling can be one of the most important parts of a person's life. The anticipation and memories that you have are some of the best. As a publisher of the Greater Than a Tourist book series, as well as the popular 50 Things to Know book series, we strive to help you learn about new places, spark your imagination, and inspire you. Wherever you are and whatever you do I wish you safe, fun, and inspiring travel.

Lisa Rusczyk Ed. D.
CZYK Publishing

GREATER THAN A TOURIST SERIES BOOKS

Greater Than a Tourist: Australia: 250 Travel Tips from Locals

Greater Than a Tourist-Caribbean: 500 Travel Tips from Locals

Greater Than a Tourist – China : 300 Travel Tips from Locals

Greater Than a Tourist- India: 500 Travel Tips from Locals

Greater Than a Tourist-Kenya: 300 Travel Tips from Locals

Greater Than a Tourist - ITALY: 400 Travel Tips from Locals

Greater than a Tourist- Pakistan: 250 Travel Tips from a Locals

Greater Than a Tourist- Romania: 250 Travel Tips from Locals

Greater Than a Tourist- Serbia: 250 Travel Tips from a Locals

Greater Than a Tourist- Spain: 350 Travel Tips from Locals

Greater Than a Tourist- South Africa: 300 Travel Tips from Locals

>TOURIST

WELCOME TO
> TOURIST

>TOURIST

Greater Than a Tourist – Cape Town South Africa

50 Travel Tips from a Local

Mia Masson

DEDICATION

This book is dedicated to my husband, Guillaume, who might be the only person who loves Cape Town more than I do. Here's to all our future adventures together, mon amour!

ABOUT THE AUTHOR

Mia Masson is a South African who lives in Paris, France, where she works as a writer. She loves animals, travel and cooking. She lived in and around Cape Town from the age of 15 to 22, studying at the University of Stellenbosch and spending most weekends with her friends in Cape Town. She considers herself an expert on finding the best places to enjoy a sundowner in her favourite city. In this seaside city of 3,7 million people, Mia feels at home.

She finds Capetonians to be relaxed, friendly and trendy people who love their food. So much so, that Cape Town is one of the most innovative cities when it comes to food and drink. Every month, countless new restaurants and bars open, reflecting the ever-changing taste of the cool Capetonians.

Another aspect of the Mother City that Mia loves is the art and design scene. Cape Town was chosen as the World Design Capital in 2014, and the art scene has exploded recently. With family members working in the art field, she knows some of the best places in the city to experience local up-and-coming artists and designers.

Mia loves living in Paris (who wouldn't?!) but a piece of her heart will always be in Cape Town, the friendliest and most beautiful place in the entire world. Fortunately, her French husband has also been bitten by the Cape Town bug so going back to visit is never a problem!

HOW TO USE THIS BOOK

This book was written by someone who has lived in an area for over three months. The author has made the best suggestions based on their own experiences in the area. Please check that these places are still available before traveling to the area. The goal of this book is to help travellers either dream or experience different locations by providing opinions from a local.

>TOURIST

The most important step to take before planning your travels is to get yourself acquainted with the map of the city. Without knowing what lies where, how will you know where to stay? So as an introduction to this book, I implore you to have a look at Cape Town's map and discover where to find the ocean, the mountain, the CBD and the airport. Once you've orientated yourself, you can start looking for accommodation. My preferred websites include AirBnb, Booking and Safari Now.

There are many luxurious and world-class hotels in Cape Town, including the Ritz, which is newly renovated, the One and Only Hotel, the Marriott and the Twelve Apostles.

We also have a culture of bed and breakfasts in South Africa, so you won't have to look far to find a B&B that is great value for money.

If you're looking for a more authentic, local experience, however, I suggest renting an apartment on AirBnb or any similar website, which allows you to experience the city the way a local does. After all, that's what this book is about, isn't it?

The best neighbourhoods to look out for, if you're planning on renting an independent apartment, include Tamboerskloof, CBD, Sea Point, Woodstock, De Waterkant and Gardens.

These neighbourhoods are all close to many of the great places I mention in this book and close to public transport, the My Citi Bus, too. The currency used in South Africa is the Rand (R), and there are eleven official languages, of which English is one.

1. HIKE UP THE MOUNTAIN

Whether you are the adventurous type or not, there is a hike for everyone. Being on top of the mountain will give you a great vantage point of Cape Town, making it easier to orientate yourself and making for some of the most beautiful photos for your album cover. There are always people hiking up Table Mountain and Lion's Head, so you are unlikely to find yourself alone and lost. Fellow hikers are always friendly and willing to offer a helping hand or guidance. However, always hike in a group and remember water, sunscreen and your camera.

The Lion's Head hike takes only about two hours and is relatively easy. Go early in the morning or on a full moon evening – you will be bound to find crowds of people enjoying a bottle of wine at the top under the full moon.

The Table Mountain hike is more challenging and takes about five hours, but you have the option of buying a ticket to take the cableway down.

Either way, this hike will be one of your favourite moments in Cape Town!

>TOURIST

2. EAT THE BEST FISH AND CHIPS OF YOUR LIFE

Kalk Bay is an old fishing village next to Cape Town, famous for its seafood and art galleries. The public train passes through the village from the CBD, and makes for a fun day outing.

Kalky's at the harbour is a spot adored by the locals and well-known for its no-nonsense, old-fashioned fish and chips. Served in enormous portions for very reasonable prices, it's no wonder people flock from near and far to try the famous Kalky's.

The dishes are served in cardboard boxes and wrapped in newsprint, adding to the authentic feel of the place. It is not fine dining, but there is a reason that Kalky's is considered the best by all the locals.

You can get a full meal including fish, chips, calamari, prawns and rolls in the form of a platter, serving two or three people, for a very reasonable price. They also offer cheap beers and soft drinks.

Treat yourself to stunning views on the quaint harbour and savour the salty air while feasting on more fresh fish than you can manage.

3. GO WINE TASTING ON A MOUNTAIN

The 330-year-old wine estate built on the slopes of Table Mountain has a history almost as rich as its wines. Commander Simon Van Der Stel, a Dutch settler with an extensive knowledge of viticulture, arrived in Cape Town in the 1600s and founded what we know today as Great Constantia Wine Estate.

South African wines have been winning international awards for many years, and no trip to the country would be complete without tasting some of those famous wines. At Great Constantia, you can treat yourself to a tasting of five wines and a cellar tour for R100, and stay as long as you want enjoying the view over Cape Town. Many locals go there over the weekend to be outside in the fresh air and enjoy each other's company.

One of the best aspects of wine farms in the region is that they attract all kinds of locals and tourists because of the reasonable prices. Everyone, from students with tight budgets, to wealthy businessmen and tourists spend their time sipping on world-class wines in front of the city scape.

4. GO SHOPPING LIKE A LOCAL

While most tour guides direct tourists straight to the V&A Waterfront for shopping, locals are more likely to go to the famous Long Street. If you're looking for designer brands, vintage clothing, interior decoration and bargain buys, you will find them all in one straight line.

Long Street is a platform for emerging and established local designers, so you can be sure that shopping there gives you the best of what the country has to offer.

>TOURIST

A List, WAG, So You, Afraid of Mice, Me Me Me, David West, Mungo and Jemima and Sitting Pretty are some of the great boutiques whose clientele range from South African celebrities looking for red carpet outfits to local students searching for bargain vintage clothes.

5. TAKE A CRUISE IN THE BAY

The iconic view of Table Mountain is best seen from the bay, and the best way to experience it is by taking a cruise on a boat at sunset.

The Peroni Catamaran departs at around 18:30 in Table Bay, depending on the season, and the ticket price includes complimentary champagne. Get a group of friends together, of opt for a romantic couple cruise, and feel rich and famous for an evening.

Many locals rent out these boats for birthday parties or corporate events, as the view is truly special.

6. HUNT FOR VINTAGE VINYLS

If you're a music lover, a collector of old records or simply enjoy window shopping, the Cape Town music scene will not disappoint.

The famous Rodriguez, whose story is as bizarre as it is moving, became famous in South Africa and his album, Cold Fact, was extremely popular. It was a Capetonian from Mabu Vinyl Store who participated in the Academy Award-winning documentary, Searching for Sugar Man.

Mabu houses an incredible collection of original records in pristine condition. You might also want to check out Kandi Records, Vinyl Cafe and Deer Hunter.

You can grab a takeaway coffee and spend your morning browsing endless collections of some of the most legendary old (and new) music, and take home a thoughtful souvenir.

7. ENJOY LIVE MUSIC UNDER THE STARS

If you happen to be passing through Cape Town during summer, you do not want to miss out on the opportunity to watch a live, open-air music concert in the botanical gardens.

Kirstenbosch Gardens hosts the Summer Sunset Concerts series every year from November through to April, and there is a wide variety of musicians and artists that are set to perform each Sunday.

The open-air amphitheatre is set to a backdrop of Table Mountain and surrounded by tall trees, making you forget that you're in a city.

Pack a picnic basket with some good South Africa wine, snacks and a blanket (not forgetting a jacket in case it gets chilly later on in the evening), and arrive early to find a good spot on the grass in front of the stage.

This event is a hit with the locals and is full every singe Sunday, so be sure to reserve your tickets in advance.

8. BREAK YOUR FAST THE CAPE TOWN WAY

Capetonians are big on breakfast. As a city that rises early, breakfast dates are not uncommon and even people that have full-time jobs meet their friends for a coffee and a bite before heading off for the day.

Two of the most famous and busy places around breakfast time are Jarryd's in Sea Point and Jason's in Bree Street. You have to go early to get a table, but this means that you'll get the warm bread, sweet cronuts and crispy pastries as they come out of the oven. South African love a good old spin on the traditional English breakfast, so you'll find all kinds of options including eggs, bacon and toast. Most places have gluten-free, vegan and vegetarian options on the menu.

Knead Bakery in Kloof Street, Baked in Camps Bay and Superette in Woodstock are well-loved for their extensive breakfast menus.

Start your day early the Cape Town way and don't forget, breakfast is the most important meal of the day!

9. GO HORSE RIDING ON ONE OF THE PRISTINE BEACHES

Whether you are an experienced rider looking for a new challenge or an adventure-seeker who just loves to experience new things, you will be welcome at Noordhoek beach.

Imhoff Equestrian Centre in Kommetjie offers three rides a day along the incredible Cape Town beaches, and the guides take on all levels of riders.

Galloping along between the sea and the mountains, feeling the salty breeze on your face and meeting locals who have lived in Cape Town all their lives will add a super experience to your holiday.

Be sure to make a booking on the website, and don't forget sunblock and comfortable trainers.

10. DRIVE ALONG THE WORLD'S MOST BEAUTIFUL COASTAL ROAD

Chapman's Peak Drive has been voted the world's most beautiful coastal drive by various publications, and for good reason. Rent a car or hop on the big, red City Sightseeing bus, which also has a route along the pass, and head from Cape Town over the mountains to Fish Hoek.

Before you set off, check the website to see the road status, as it is sometimes closed due to rock falls. There is also a tollgate where one has to pay an entrance fee for the upkeep of the world-famous pass, but the trip is worth it.

You will not be disappointed by the amazing lookout points which make for some of the most famous photos of Cape Town, and you can feel like a professional photographer yourself.

>TOURIST

"This cape is the most stately thing and the fairest cape we saw in the whole circumference of the earth."

– From the journal of Sir Francis Drake, on seeing the Cape for the first time, 1580

11. SPEND A DAY AT THE WATERFRONT

The Victoria & Alfred Waterfront is always a good choice, come rain or shine. It is a family-friendly environment with exceptional restaurants, world-class shopping and extensive entertainment activities. Locals love to pop into the waterfront for a quick lunch or coffee to accompany their shopping, but you needn't be that rushed. Take time to wander through the V&A Food Market, a permanent undercover market made up of around 30 different stalls, selling street food from the four corners of the earth, artisan coffee blends, local beverages and freshly-pressed juices.

When you're ready for a glass of wine or a cocktail next to the water, head to the Grand Café, right next door. There are metre-long pizzas and imaginative cocktails, and you sit with your feet in the sand, staring out at the yachts on the bay.

The Waterfront has two cinemas, hundreds of shops and restaurants, and play areas for the kids. There is also an outdoor amphitheatre for live music and sports broadcastings, and from the port you can go for a sail around the harbour or buy tickets to dive with sharks, go on a helicopter ride or paraglide off the mountain. You can also experience our own version of the London Eye and go on the big Ferris wheel with a view of the city. Capetonians go to the waterfront all year long, so you will get a true local feel.

12. TAKE A TRIP INTO THE COUNTRY'S FAMOUS HISTORY

South Africa went through a famously terrible period, Apartheid, during the 1900s. It would be wise to read up a little about the segregation before your trip, but if you are interested in knowing even more about it, you should visit the District Six Museum. It is the lesser-known of the museums in Cape Town, but one of the most informative and moving.

You will feel the presence of the coloured and black people who were forcefully removed from their beloved homes, having their families broken up by the white government.

The museum is designed in such a way that you will feel as if you're walking in the streets of the famous neighbourhood. Entrance is reasonable and you can try some traditional, Cape Malay snacks at the end of the visit. This is one historical and educational experience that will tell you more detail about the Rainbow Nation's troubled past, and you won't be surrounded by tourists.

>TOURIST

13. DISCOVER A SECRET BAR HIDDEN FROM THE STREET

Nothing says "local" better than knowing the places that are hidden from street view. The Honest Chocolate gin bar is such a well-kept secret that many locals don't even know about it.

When passing by on Wale street, you will see a lovely, tempting chocolate bar that serves tarts, pastries and hot chocolate. But if you follow your nose to the back of the shop and continue through the little door, you will find yourself in a little courtyard with plants hanging from the walls, fairy lights and a glass door leading into the bar.

You need to have a taste for gin, or at least a sense of adventure to try a new drink, because their combinations are out of their world. Try a basil gin and tonic, or one with strawberries and cinnamon. For the beer drinkers, there is a variety of beer available, too.

This place gets going on the weekends and on a Wednesday evening. You will be sure to only meet locals among the young, hip crowd.

14. SHOP IN AN OLD FISH FACTORY

If you take a little drive over the mountain, you will find yourself in Hout Bay, a fishing town with a harbour and local seals who lie on the beach tanning all day.

Every Friday night and Saturday and Sunday morning, the Bay Market comes to life in an authentic former fish factory, right on the harbour, and local vendors set up their stalls. You can find great South African fashion, décor and a lot of antique furniture.

Not that any Cape Town market would be complete without food, of course, and you can find numerous famous chefs cooking up fresh seafood, dry-aged steak sandwiches and generous salads. There is also no lack of craft beer.

Listening to some live jazz music punctured by the squawking of seagulls while browsing the market with friends is one of the best ways to spend a Sunday morning in Cape Town.

15. TRY YOUR HAND AT A NEW SPORT IN THE HARBOUR

Stand Up Paddle Boarding (SUP) is one of the latest sport trends to grip Capetonians. It involves keeping your balance on a long, thick board whilst paddling, and it's great fun. Anyone can do it, too; you don't have to be a professional surfer!

The Cape Town SUP Clubhouse rents out boards for short- or long-term use during summer, and they also give lessons on Clifton beach, where they are always stationed under a Bedouin tent. If you're feeling brave, join their Thursday night City Slickers challenge – you go into the water with a big group of fellow adventure seekers when it's dark!

SUP is a fun activity for the whole family, and so many locals have become really good at it and go out every week. It embodies the spirit of Capetonians, who love being outside in nature, having fun and trying new things.

You can check online if you're unsure about the weather, as the clubhouse sometimes closes due to rain or wind.

16. SIP ON AFTERNOON TEA LIKE A ROYAL

A favourite outing for special occasions is having high tea at the Belmond Mount Nelson hotel. The historical monument was opened in 1899 by English settlers, and was the first hotel in the country to have hot and cold running water.

Famous guests at South Africa's most ancient and iconic luxury hotel include Oprah Winfrey, Winston Churchill, the Dalai Lama, Tiger Woods and Lenny Kravitz.

You can pretend you're a royal for a day and enjoy high tea in the opulent tea room. You will enjoy finger sandwiches of roast beef, salmon or cucumber, followed by sticky lemon meringue or dark chocolate cake, and accompanied by mini pastries, macarons, scones with clotted cream and a traditional South African dessert, milk tart.

High tea at the Mount Nelson is very reasonably priced, so there is no excuse to skip this gorgeous setting if you're celebrating an anniversary, a girls' afternoon, a birthday or simply a great trip to Cape Town.

17. SEE A SHOW AT A LEGENDARY THEATRE

The Fugard Theatre is one of the most iconic spaces that fought against the apartheid government with art during the darkest years.

Athol Fugard is the country's greatest living playwright, a man who was ahead of his time and was able to see through the inhumane segregationist policies of the time and risked his life and his freedom to give a voice to the oppressed.

The theatre continues to be an icon, showing plays that fight the system, tell tales of our history and create awareness amongst the audience.

You probably won't see any tourists on an average evening at the theatre, and that's the best part – you will find yourself in Cape Town's heart and soul.

18. TELEPORT TO A STEAMPUNK COFFEE PARADISE

Cape Town has a coffee culture different to that of Paris or Rome, but in my opinion, much more interesting. Artisan coffee brewers started popping up recently and the industry has become a booming success, thanks to the innovative mindset of Capetonians.

In Cape Town, you don't just order your black coffee to go; it's an art there. From cappuccinos to cortados, you've got to know the difference between all the brews and between all the rival coffee

>TOURIST

shops. Some of the greatest coffee shops include Tribe, Haas, Flat Mountain and Deluxe, there is only one king.

Truth Coffee Shop has been voted the best coffee shop in the world by The Telegraph for the second consecutive year, and is truly impressive. Besides the obviously incredible variety and quality of coffee, the interior of the shops makes you feel like you've been transported to another world. A steampunk paradise. Waiters and baristas are dressed in Mad Max-esque outfits with googles and leather waistcoats, and the copper bars and chairs are full of nuts and bolts. There is an enormous, old coffee machine that has so many pipes it looks like a church organ. Dive into the heart of Cape Town's coffee culture and buy a bag to take home, because I can guarantee that you will want something to remember this moment by.

19. TAKE YOUR TASTEBUDS ON A JOYRIDE

South African cuisine is greatly influenced by Eastern flavours, due to slaves that were imported from the East during the colonial times. The Eastern Food Bazaar is one of Cape Town's most visited food markets. It is not expensive, it is not fancy, it is not well-known by tourists and it is not luxurious, but you will find some of the best Eastern cuisine you've tasted in your life.

Order from the long counters and sit down at plastic chairs and tables, surrounded by all kinds of Capetonians, from the poorer population to young students, to wealthy businesspeople taking a lunch break. This indoor market brings together people from all backgrounds in search of the same thing – big portions of authentic, spicy food.

Good luck choosing between true North Indian curries, traditional Cape Malay boboties that are found in the Bo-Kaap neighbourhood, Turkish kebabs and authentic shawarmas and falafels.

20. TAKE IN THE CITY'S BEST VIEWS FROM THE BEST ROOFTOPS

There are a few rooftop bars worth mentioning in Cape Town, such as the Tjing Tjing bar in Longmarket Street, Yours Truly in Kloof Street and the bar of the Grand Daddy Hotel in Long Street. But the newest addition to Cape Town's nightlife and perhaps the most luxurious one is the Willaston Bar at the Silo Hotel.

Enjoy classic cocktails or Cape wine with views of the sea, the harbour and the industrial city centre.

Open-air bars are always full, unless it's raining, as Capetonians love looking at views of their city. Be sure to find out about happy hours and specials at these bars, as you can usually get great deals if you go early – and an added bonus is that you can watch the sun set over the sea.

>TOURIST

> *"During the many years of incarceration on Robben Island, we often looked across Table Mountain at its magnificent silhouette ... To us on Robben Island, Table Mountain was a beacon of hope. It represented the mainland to which we knew we would one day return."*
>
> – Former President Nelson Mandela

21. RIDE TO THE TOP OF TABLE MOUNTAIN

Cape Town's oldest, most famous and most beloved landmark is our flat mountain that looks like a table. Formed thousands of years ago, it looms over the city like a great protector.

The sight of Table Mountain is famous throughout the world and can be seen from almost anywhere in the city. If you want to get an idea of what our "protector" sees when she's looking down on us, take the cable car to the top and you will see the city sprawled out below you.

You can buy a ticket online and also make sure that the cableway is running that day, as it closes in cases of strong winds. Remember to take a warm jacket, even in summer, as the air is much colder at 1800m above sea level.

When you get to the top, the view will leave you breathless. You can see the entire map of Cape Town, from the Atlantic sea board to the flat Woodstock and the highways leaving the city. You can see the famous Robben Island where Nelson Mandela was imprisoned, approximately 12km off the coast, and you'll see boats and airplanes. Due to the flatness of the mountain's surface, you can walk the entire summit without getting too tired.

Watch out for the adorable little dassies, which are small mountain creatures that look like squirrels, and are always begging for food!

You will also experience on top of Table Mountain, one of the richest floral kingdoms in the world. It is said that there are more different species of plants on Table Mountain alone that in the whole of England.

Fynbos is the plant type that is endemic to the region, meaning it grows nowhere else in the entire world. Fynbos is home to many animal, bird and insect species that also exist nowhere else in the world. Your ticket to the top of the mountain helps maintain and protect their home.

22. TAKE A STROLL ALONG THE PROMENADE

All true Capetonians spend their mornings walking, running or strolling along the Sea Point promenade with their babies in prams, dogs on leashes or families. The well-maintained stretch of pavement runs right next to the sea, making for inspiring views and fresh air as you take your walk.

It stretches for 11km all the way from Sea Point to Mouille Point, right near the V&A Waterfront. Walking along the promenade, you can see the ocean, the mountains and the beautiful, old Cape Dutch buildings. The noise of the waves and the salty taste of the air, as well as the seagulls squawking above you, will make you feel close to nature even in such a big city.

For children, there are jungle gyms, swings and slides all along the green park the stretches next to the promenade, and for the fun, outdoorsy type, there is an outdoor gym that is free. You can train right next to the ocean with your friends halfway through your cardio workout! There are also little benches every few metres, that double as works of art, with hopeful and inspiring messages for the people of Cape Town.

23. GLAM UP YOUR EVENING WITH COCKTAILS NEXT TO THE BEACH

Camps Bay's Victoria Street has long been famous for attracting the rich and famous of the Mother City. Countless bars, clubs and restaurants line her strip and from all of them, you can see the sun set over the sea.

However, this neighbourhood is not reserved for the glitzy locals – anyone can enjoy sundowners in Camps Bay because of the wide variety of establishments. If you have spent the day on the idyllic Camps Bay beach and come to a café wearing flip-flops and a dress over your swimming costume, you will be welcomed with open arms. If you're looking for something a little more classy, trade the bikini for a dress and get to Café Caprice early to skip the queues, and enjoy rubbing shoulders with South Africa's hottest party-goers.

The best thing about this stretch of road is that Sunday nights are usually the busiest in summer, which means that even if everything in the city bowl is closed, the party is happening next to the beach. You can see the beach and the big boulders from the pavements of all the bars, and watching the sky turn pink after a Camps Bay sunset is something that each visitor has to experience.

24. VISIT THE PRISON CELL WHERE MANDELA WAS INCARCERATED

One of South Africa's most precious and beloved personalities was Nelson Rolihlahla Mandela. The former president and political activist spent 27 years in prison for opposing the evil apartheid government, and for 18 years he was incarcerated on the famous Robben Island.

This island lies 12km off the coast of Cape Town and the only way to access it is by ferry. The ticket office and departure point is at the V&A Waterfront, where you will find all the information you need regarding times and tariffs.

Mandela and his fellow political prisoners spent years looking over the sea to the Motherland, and when they saw Table Mountain they claimed to find hope, because they knew that life was still going on and that one day they, too, would join the population. The hardest part about being imprisoned on Robben Island, however, was that their families and friends, real life, the government was only a few kilometres away across the sea – so close, yet so out of reach for the prisoners.

>TOURIST

The visit to the former prison is one that will change your life and move you to tears. Learn about Mandela's life and those of his friends, Robert Sobukwe and Walter Sisulu. You will see the tiny cell where Mandela spent 18 years cramped and sleeping on the floor, where he found enough inspiration to write his novel, A Long Walk To Freedom, and where he continued to study and fight for the rights of black South Africans.

What makes the Robben Island museum so unique and touching is that all the tour guides on the island are former prisoners. You will hear a first-hand account of what life was in there during apartheid. It is a truly incredible and memorable experience, for tourists and locals alike.

25. CULTIVATE YOUR ART TASTE THE LOCAL WAY

Count yourself lucky if you happen to be in the Mother City on the first Thursday of each month. Art galleries and cultural attractions are open until late, and bars are overflowing onto the sidewalks.

First Thursdays is open to everyone and is free to attend, allowing visitors to tour the cultural landmarks by foot in the City Bowl. There is no tour guide or schedule, so you can look at the website for more specific locations and maps, but mostly you will see hordes of people ambling along the pavements, going from gallery to bar to shop to cinema. All the stops also give away free printed maps, in case you feel overwhelmed by the crowds or choices of spots to visit.

This event is becoming more popular every month, and is already very well-known among the locals. Enjoy the art, the live music, the pop-up shops and South African designers as well as the best local talent Cape Town has to offer in a casual setting. No-one will even know you're a tourist!

26. PLAY WITH WILD PENGUINS

Boulders Beach, named after the huge granite boulders that protect it from the sea, is situated near Simon's Town and Kalk Bay, and forms part of the Table Mountain National Park, a protected area. In 1982, a colony of African penguins settled there, and they still live there today, protected, happy and free.

It's truly an amazing experience to walk up onto the beach and see hundreds of wild penguins tanning on the rocks, diving into the ice cold water and playing with each other. One of the attractions that makes South Africa so special and popular is that one can see animals in their natural habitat, not in a zoo or in cages.

There are nearly 3000 penguins on Boulders Beach, and as this species is classified as vulnerable to extinction, it's a beautiful thing to see them in a protected but free environment.

It's a fun idea to pack a picnic basket, throw on your swimming costume and head to Boulders Beach for the day. From there you can access the wheelchair-friendly wooden boardwalk that takes you all along the beach and allows you to see hundreds of penguins playing in the water.

>TOURIST

27. TAKE A TRIP THROUGH THE TOWNSHIP

Khayelitsha and Gugulethu are some of the most interesting and authentic parts of Cape Town and its history. The townships, which were created after the apartheid government forcefully removed people of colour from their homes in the city and displaced them in the outskirts, still represent poverty and a colonial legacy today. However, it is in the heart of the townships that you will discover the true meaning of South Africa's rainbow nation. People are happy, smiling, full of energy and motivation and joy, despite their tough circumstances. A walking tour through the township with a knowledgeable guide can open your eyes to how the majority of the poorer population live.

You will discover traditional cuisine, some great coffee shops that give all proceeds to improving the community and a wonderful bed & breakfast where the owner's objective is to make tourists feel comfortable and erase the stigma of township danger. I advise you not to go on this tour with the spirit of a tourist, but rather with a genuine interest in getting to know the culture and personalities of the people living in these rough conditions. There is no doubt that they will put a smile on your face and when you see how lovely these people are, you will realise why Nelson Mandela managed to orchestrate a peaceful transition of power after apartheid – because it took a little bit of hope, a lot of courage and a spirit of reconciliation.

28. SPEND A DAY IN THE WINELANDS

Stellenbosch is a historical town located just 45 minutes from Cape Town along the N1 or N2 highway. No trip to this fabulous wine region is complete without capitalising on the excellent wine sold at incredible retail prices on the estates themselves. There are so many reasons to visit Stellenbosch, including the natural beauty of the rolling vines, the blue mountains, the historical buildings, the world-class wine and the mouth-watering food. Nowhere else in the world will you find such a collection of vineyards that allow visitors to have just one glass of wine, or do a tasting of 5 different wines, at such a reasonable price, without being obliged to buy a crate.

Among the most impressive estates are Ernie Els and Guardian Peak, Beyerskloof, Kanonkop, Jordan, Boschendal, Lanzerac, Rust en Vrede, Lourensford, Bartinney, Tokara and Delaire Graaff. At any of them you will be able to do a wine tasting, order a bottle or a glass of wine, and eat a hearty meal.

Be sure to try the Pinotage wine, a South African cultivar that was created by accident by a South African winemaker, is made nowhere else in the world and has won numerous international awards. If you are unsure of where to start, visit the tourism office at the top of Church Street in Stellenbosch. There, you will find information about all the surrounding wine farms, transport options and other visits.

>TOURIST

29. GET LOST IN THE MOST BEAUTIFUL GARDEN IN AFRICA

The Kirstenbosch National Botanical Garden lives up to its acclaim as Africa's most beautiful garden. Set on the slopes of Table Mountain, the garden was established in 1913 to conserve and promote the rich biodiversity.

Cape Town is often named the most biodiverse city in the world, and the Kirstenbosch Gardens protect over 7000 species of plants, including the "fynbos" that is endemic to this region. The Cape Floral Kingdom was named a UNESCO World Heritage Site in 2004, giving the gardens even more credibility.

You can either do a free walking tour, or pack a picnic and set up your blankets under the trees. The Boomslang (tree snake), a wooden treetop walkway, is an absolute must. You can walk for 130m through the canopy of tree tops, as if you were walking on their leaves, with a view of the mountain, the gardens and the adjacent suburbs.

Locals love to go to Kirstenbosch for open-air concerts, picnics and walks any day of the week.

30. DINE AT SOUTH AFRICA'S BEST RESTAURANT

If you really want to treat yourself during your trip to Cape Town, The Test Kitchen is the place to go.

It has won the prestigious award of South Africa's best restaurant every year since 2012, and has been included in the Top 50 Restaurants in the world, most recently as number 22 on the list in 2016.

The restaurant is set in the Old Biscuit Mill, Woodstock, giving it an extremely authentic and hipster feel, even though it is so prestigious. That's the amazing thing about Cape Town – you have a mix of old and new wherever you look.

The atmosphere is modern, warm and welcoming, and the service is top-notch. You will want to order everything off the menu, and the wine list is also impressive, boasting mostly local wines with a selection of international wines, too.

It is a truly special experience and you have to book weeks in advance to get a table, but if you do, you will experience the pinnacle of Cape Town cuisine, and realise why the world is celebrating the Mother City as being one of the most innovative gastronomic places in the world.

"I've learnt to see Africa with new eyes, from the perspective of a continent that has given the world so much, that has nourished it like a mother nourishes her child. A continent full of colours, feelings, smiles, and kids with enormous talent that are just waiting for the chance to shine (...) I wasn't surprised to find so much beauty, but I

>TOURIST

never expected to see such warm, gentle and loving people; I had never been given that much love, that many hugs and kisses, that many smiles. That is what makes me believe in humankind over and over again"

– Shakira, singer

31. HIT THE SURF AT AN ICONIC BEACH

Muizenberg might be famous for its gorgeous, colourful cabins that line the beach and are a travel blogger's favourite place to take photos, but the surfers will tell you other stories about this beach.

The gentle, sloping white beach and freezing cold water is home to some of the best waves around Cape Town, and it's a perfect spot for beginners.

There are no rocks in Muizenberg's beach break, making it safe and easy to jump on a long board and get learning.

Gary's Surf School is one of the best-known instruction centers in the area, and you can find all the information on their website.

Capetonians love surfing and many locals surf in the morning before work, as well as in the late afternoon after work, and all weekend long. A city that is so close to the water is bound to have a large population of adventurers doing water sports every day of the week!

32. FILL YOUR SOUL AT THE LOCALS' FAVOURITE INDOOR MARKET

The Neighbour Goods Market has become an institution in Cape Town and Johannesburg, where there is a sister market on the city's rooftops. The Capetonians flock to the Old Biscuit Mill early on Saturday mornings, throughout the year, come rain or shine.

On the food side, this market is not lacking – you can have your fill of traditional African cuisine, creative snacks such as mushroom kebabs, locally produced fresh goods and ample bars to choose from. People often go early in the morning for breakfast and coffee with a friend, and then hang around until midday and stay for lunch and wine, as they get hungry again!

You will also find exclusively local clothes, jewellery and leather goods. These products are all of exceptional quality and will make better buys than anything you can get in chain stores.

Come prepared with an empty stomach and cash, as not all of the food stalls have card machines. You will be swept up in the sights and sounds, the live music, the flowers and fresh fruit, the sizzling food and the smoky barbecue coming at you from all directions. The Neighbour Goods market is one of the most popular outings for Capetonians of all ages and backgrounds.

>TOURIST

33. SHOP FOR ANTIQUE FURNITURE IN A NEWLY GENTRIFIED NEIGHBOURHOOD

While we're in Woodstock, we might as well go on a trip down the recently remodelled streets and buildings and hunt for antique furniture.

This neighbourhood is one of the best to find authentic antiques, dating from the olden days in South African history when the rainbow nation was still a foreign concept. You will find anything from tables and chairs to linen, mirrors and cutlery. Make your way through the small streets and you will be able to spot the antique shops with their furniture spilling out onto the pavements.

Don't hesitate to ask the owners of the shops any questions you might have regarding the age, the origin or the authenticity of their products, and you can also try and bargain with them.

A lot of Capetonians, including my own family, shop for antique furniture in Woodstock and repaint or renew them to put into a stylish, modern home. No-one is ever able to tell that the beautiful antique side table with a modern touch cost so little and was bought in such an arty part of town!

34. FEEL LIKE A KID AGAIN AND ENJOY SCOOPS BY THE SEASIDE

Summer in Cape Town is like living in a permanent movie set. The sun goes down late and the sunsets are blood orange, people are out drinking and eating every night, even during the week, and the calm sea is a beautiful blue colour.

There is nothing better than taking a long walk along the Sea Point Promenade, getting some exercise and fresh air and admiring the seagulls and the big, blue waves. But all this walking calls for a treat, and the only place to stop off at is The Creamery in Mouille Point, at the end of the promenade.

The gorgeous, pastel-coloured café will tempt you to try all their homemade ice cream flavours. With more than 60 flavours to choose from, you will definitely have a hard time making up your mind, but luckily you can also take a few tubs home so that your favourite flavours don't feel left out!

You can also try their flavour of the month that appears in their hall of fame, which is never a bad bet, and then go sit on a bench outside overlooking the sea and the pink sunset. Life doesn't get much better than that.

35. GO TO AN OLD-SCHOOL CINEMA

There is something about the "good old days" that gives a sense of comfort and wonder all at once. The Labia Theatre on Orange Street makes you feel like you're actually in one of the 1950's movies that you're about to watch.

You go inside and buy your ticket at the cute, authentic ticket booth, and it comes printed out on a small piece of pink paper, just like in the olden days. The Labia is the oldest Independent Art-

Repertory Cinema in South Africa, and has only four screens with intimate seating arrangements.

It's also the only place in Cape Town where you can have a drink at the bar and watch a movie with a glass of wine and home-baked delicacies. The cinema shows independent local and foreign films, as well as some blockbusters, but the style is rather arty.

Going to the Labia is nothing like the big-screen, big-budget cinema franchises that the world knows. It's a very intimate, friendly and cosy experience, and it's perfect to do alone or with some friends when it's a little cold outside.

36. EXPLORE CAPE TOWN'S VIBRANT ART SCENE

Art has always been an important part of South Africa's history, from being used way back by the indigenous Khoi and San people, who painted on rocks in caves, to expressing political outrage during the times of apartheid.

The Goodman Gallery was established in Johannesburg in 1966, and has a history of promoting local artists who are influential and contemporary, telling the story of South Africa today. It was one of the first spaces that offered a non-discriminatory exhibition space, fighting back against the racist government through self-expression. You can look on the website to find out which temporary exhibitions will be on show at the time of your trip.

Entrance is free to this iconic institution, and it's open from Tuesday through Saturday.

Be prepared to be inspired, to be moved and to learn about the openness of the new South Africa in what is probably the most influential contemporary art space in Africa.

37. GO FIND THE MOST FAMOUS VIEW OF THE MOUNTAIN

One of the best drives to take around Cape Town is to Bloubergstrand (blue mountain beach), named after the way Table Mountain appears blue after sunset. If you search Table Mountain on Google, the first images that pop up are surely ones taken from Bloubergstrand.

If you would like to take in this view for a bit longer, head over to the Blue Peter Hotel and order a bottle of wine and a pizza at the restaurant. You can sit outside on the grass while enjoying it, and from there you can see the mountain in all its glory.

Many locals frequent this establishment over weekends at sunset time, and the atmosphere is very vibrant and lively. Music, views and good wine, being surrounded by locals and living like a real Capetonian should all be on your Cape Town bucket list.

The Blue Peter restaurant is not known for fine dining, but rather for a laid-back, casual atmosphere and the view. If this is what you're looking for, you'll love it.

>TOURIST

38. SUPPORT LOCAL DESIGNERS

The Watershed at the V&A Waterfront is the ultimate South African design destination in Cape Town. In this enormous indoor marketplace you will find around 150 local vendors who represent more than 365 brands of clothing, décor, jewellery, art and other crafts.

The Jubilee Exhibition Hall also houses temporary exhibitions, art works, concerts and more, so find out on the website what's showing during your trip to Cape Town.

A lot of tourists want to take souvenirs to their families back home, without looking like a total tourists. The Watershed is just the place for that, because the local designers create such beautiful and authentic products that even locals shop there all the time.

Not only can you buy high-quality South African products, but you can also treat yourself to a range of beauty and health treatments at the Wellness at the Watershed section on the ground floor. Capetonians love to stop off at the Watershed on a trip to the Waterfront, because there is always something new to see and buy. It's an exciting environment that allows you to support local designers and craftspeople, most of whom come from difficult backgrounds and poverty, so it's a wonderful way to give back to the community.

39. SEE WHY EVERYONE IS GOING VEGAN

Cape Town is a city that is more healthy and active than most. Being so close to nature seems to inspire Capetonians to enjoy outdoor activities and sports, and this lifestyle inspires a healthy diet. They seem to all have glowing skin and lots of energy, and some say it's because of the fresh air and their proximity with Mother Nature.

Many Capetonians are vegan or vegetarian, and even those that aren't can often be spotted dining at the city's growing number of healthy eateries, because the food is so good that even meat lovers don't miss meat.

Why not see for yourself what the craze is about and visit some of Cape Town's hottest, healthiest eateries?

Sexy Food in Bree Street lets you build your own lunch, Scheckter's Raw in Regent Street will heal your mind and body with their soul food, and Plant Café in Buiten Street donates part of its proceeds to animal charities. Zucchini's in Loop Street makes amazing, guilt-free sweet treats and Hungry Herbivore in Orphan Street promises healthy comfort food that should leave you feeling good. Captonians are constantly seen grabbing lunch or a detox juice at one of these cool eateries, so if you really want to feel like a local you should try it – guilt free!

>TOURIST

40. LAUGH UNTIL YOU CRY AT THE COMEDY CLUB

The Cape Town Comedy Club features among the Top 10 Comedy Clubs in the world on Traveller, so this is one outing that you don't want to miss. They say there is no better way to understand a person than through their sense of humour, and South African comedy is a very particular brand. The iconic club started in 2005 as a temporary pop-up show for a festival, but when it was a huge success, the founder told himself that this needed to be permanent. And so Capetonians started including comedy shows into their monthly agendas, supporting local talent and finding ways to laugh at the country's sad political state.

The hall is set in The Pumphouse at the V&A Waterfront, a building that dates back to 1882 and was used to pump water from the world's oldest dock in operation. Today, it is an eclectic club mixing comedy, cheap drinks and a South African atmosphere that is hard to come by anywhere else.

The comedians love to joke about our country's politics, using satire as a weapon to send a message of protest, and this method is one that has been cultivated and perfected in South Africa since the times of apartheid. If you are interested in understanding the people, the history, the pains and the laughs of Capetonians, the Cape Town Comedy Club is just the place that will open doors for you.

"Cape Town is incredible and it deserves all the attention it's getting. Not only does it have staggering natural beauty—mountains, beaches—

it also has an incredible lifestyle. Great wine, food, design, culture—you name it, Cape Town has it."

- Vogue magazine

41. FOLLOW YOUR NOSE

The Bo-Kaap is one of the most iconic neighbourhoods, lying on the slopes of the Signal Hill and livening up the city's landscape with its multi-coloured houses. Tourists love to take photos of the beautiful architecture, but you're trying to experience it more like a local – and that's why you need to look into the Bo-Kaap Cooking Tour. The Cape Malay community that predominantly resides there arrived in Cape Town as slaves from Indonesia in the time that both countries were a Dutch colony. The neighbourhood has long been home to Cape Town's Muslim community as people of colour were forced to move there under the apartheid government's Group Areas Act. However, today, the greatest threat facing the neighbourhood is gentrification.

Europeans and other travellers have noticed the beauty and real estate potential of the Bo-Kaap and have started buying up old houses and remodelling them. This is why the residents are fighting to keep their traditions, their culture, their religion and their food. The cooking class takes place at Zainia's home, where she will teach you to make the Cape Malay cuisine which South Africans adore. You will learn to make samosas, curries and how to mix an incredible number of spices. Be sure to take some spices and recipes

>TOURIST

home with you to impress your friends and family with your authentic South African cooking skills.

42. GET YOUR TOES WET AT AN ICONIC BEACH

Cape Town is known for its pristine, white-sand beaches that attract celebrities from all over the world.

Camps Bay is a great beach for swimming (if you're not afraid of cold water!), playing bats and balls or soccer and taking long walks. It is a family-friendly beach that is always busy!

But if you're looking for something a little more secluded, sexy and pristine, head over to Clifton. There are four beaches in Clifton, separated by large, smooth boulders and you can walk along the sand until you reach the last one. Here, you will find couples on a romantic holiday, groups of friends having picnics and famous people hiding under hats and large sunglasses.

This stretch of land is one of the most expensive real estate areas in Africa, and it's easy to see why. Beautiful apartments and enormous mansions line the beach and beautiful people walk along the sand. It's one of the places in Cape Town where you can truly feel like a celebrity. The water is ice cold, but a beautiful blue colour, so a quick swim to cool you off after hours of tanning is encouraged. Capetonians adore Clifton because it's clean, protected, beautiful and right on their doorstep. There are also some great cocktail bars and restaurants nearby which are perfect for sundowners after a day on the beach.

43. TASTE CRAFT BEERS IN A HISTORIC STREET

Long Street is known for its vintage shops, bookstores, ethnic restaurants and bohemian bars. The architecture on the street also attracts many tourists, who love to take photos of the colourful Victorian buildings with wrought-iron railings. In Long Street, one feels Cape Town move. One sees the diversity of the city and one tastes the Rainbow Nation.

Beer House in Long Street has become an institution, always full of customers wanting to try the latest craft beer. There are 99 different types of bottled beer and 22 different types of beer on tap, making the choice a difficult one. There is also a great comfort food menu, with different specials every day of the week, such as 2 for the price of one burgers. You can get updates about their specials on Beerhouse's website.

The great thing about this pub is that it aims to promote local breweries. Although they do serve some international beers, Beerhouse gives a platform to micro-breweries where they can showcase new products and get into the commercial market. And South Africa's craft beer industry has been booming of late.

Since 2000, around 140 new micro-breweries have popped up all over the country, each one creating flavourful craft beer for the South African market. These beers have become popular amongst locals and you won't see many people drinking imported beer when they go to restaurants or bars.

>TOURIST

Taste the local beer scene and see what South Africa has managed to come up with, and prepare to be impressed.

44. JUMP OFF A MOUNTAIN

Safely, of course. We've already established that Cape Town is a city for thrill-seekers, and there is one adventure that has to be on your bucket list.

Signal Hill is situated next to Table Mountain and is easily accessible by car. It is only 350m high, but offers some thrilling views of the city. Locals love to paraglide off the top, jumping with an instructor behind them.

It is an adrenaline-inducing experience that will not only be a great story to tell your friends back home, but you are also treated to some of the city's most beautiful views from the sky. You land on the Sea Point Promenade, in front of crowds of admiring people who wish they could do what you just did. The team will even treat you to a beer afterwards, if you jump at sunset!

It's important to wear closed shoes and long pants, as well as bring a jacket and sunscreen to be safe. The team also flies with disabled people, as well as beginners. Don't be afraid to try this jump that will get your blood pumping and leave you with some great photos and a smile!

45. VISIT CAPE TOWN'S "CHURCH OF MEAT"

Before leaving South Africa, you need to experience an authentic braai (barbecue). For this occasion, you will have to venture into the township of Gugulethu. Mzoli's is a restaurant and bar found right in the middle of the corrugated-iron houses.

The owner, Mzoli, started by selling meat out of his garage in 2003, but it has since catapulted into stardom and become a meat institution loved by Capetonians and tourists alike. Only a short drive out from Cape Town into the tribal wilderness, you will find large crowds of people gathering around the bonfires and sexy house music can be heard from a distance.

Don't expect a posh restaurant – what Mzoli's offers is a rustic, authentic township feeling with top-quality meat and great grooves to get you dancing. You can stop off at a supermarket nearby and buy serviettes, paper plates and plastic cups as well as your own drinks. A few six packs of beers or some good South African red wine should do the trick.

Plastic tables are covered in blank newsprint and tourists and locals mingle like they're old friends. Get there early or reserve a table so you won't be disappointed, and stay until the music gets going. Mzoli's is the personification of the ideal Rainbow Nation, where people of all races, ages and backgrounds get along over good food.

>TOURIST

46. ALL ABOARD THE WINE TRAIN

Franschhoek is a historical town about an hour's drive from Cape Town that means "the French corner", and was founded by French Huguenots who were expelled from their country because of their religious beliefs. They brought with them to South Africa their winemaking skills and knowledge, and Franschhoek produces world-class wine even today.

Wine tourism is so big in this part of the Cape that there are many different tours available, however the most fun and valuable experience is the Franschhoek wine train. For the price of a ticket you can hop aboard a train that takes you to six different wine estates in the area, and you get a free tasting at some of them, as well as discount at others.

There are different routes to take which include different estates, but all you need to do is look up the wine farms and choose the best-looking. Dieu Donné comes highly recommended with its panoramic view of the valley, and Maison has a superb menu if you want to stop for lunch.

As you will be visiting six wine farms and sampling copious amounts of rich, South African wine, be sure to take a big bottle of water, a hat and sunblock in case it gets hot. No-one likes to mix too much wine and sunshine.

47. TREAT YOURSELF AT THE "CAKE OF GOOD HOPE"

Charly's Bakery is a sweet treat institution in Cape Town and has been given its adorable nickname by fans. They are so famous, in fact, that the owners landed their own reality TV series in 2011, Charly's Cake Angels.

This documentary series goes behind the scenes of the colourful cakes, the chocolate goodness and the marzipan icing into the lives of the family, the bakers and the community they serve. Viewers got to know the workers and the local customers, as well as the area in Cape Town where the bakery is situated.

You can visit this famous bakery in Canterbury Street and treat yourself to a mouth watering pastry. Locals love to go there on coffee and cake dates, or to get takeaways for their Sunday dessert.

Charly's is a small local business that serves in the interests of the community and has created jobs for many previously disadvantaged members of the community, giving them hope and a future. You can't go wrong when supporting this adorable family business.

48. FEED SQUIRRELS UNDER THE CITY'S OLDEST TREES

Everyone needs a break once in a while, even while you're touring a new city. Eating, drinking and exploring can exhausting and some moments call for sitting down in the shade and breathing deeply.

>TOURIST

Take a walk over to the Company's Garden in Queen Victoria Street for a breather. Originally created in the 1650s, this garden used to serve as a growing place of fresh produce for passing ships to fill up on. Today, you can still see the oldest pear tree in the country, dating back to 1652. There is also a monument commemorating the South African soldiers who lost their lives in the Great Wars, especially in the battle of Delville Wood in France, where more than 2000 South African volunteers were killed.

Under all these majestic oak trees you will see hundreds of tame squirrels scurrying about, waiting to be fed. Take some nuts or bread and stretch out your hand – they will come right up to you and eat out of your hand, making for great photos.

In the event that you feel hungry, there is a beautiful, quaint restaurant in the middle of the gardens that serves fresh dishes and good coffee. It's the perfect place to relax and regroup, and maybe update your travel journal with all of Cape Town's wonders.

49. BAR-HOP IN THE TRENDIEST PART OF TOWN

Bree Street is the enfant terrible of Cape Town when it comes to bars because there is a new one opening every few weeks, so it's impossible to keep up. You can visit so many bars and restaurants in one street that you'll feel like you've visited an entire country.

A fun way to spend an evening with your friends is to go bar-hopping along Bree Street. A lot of Cape Town locals start off (and end) their evenings this way. Everything is within walking distance of each other, so it's practical, and you can see where the crowd is moving, pointing you in the direction of the party like a human arrow.

If you start your journey at the top, begin with the Orphanage Cocktail lounge for expertly-mixed drinks. Pass by Mother's Ruin Gin Bar for an amazing locally distilled gin, and head on to Hank's Old Irish for a great pub atmosphere. Charango Bar is sure to be teeming with the after-work crowd and La Parada is full on every night of the week, thanks to its great big bar and Spanish-inspired tapas list.

You will be bumping into locals left and right and get a better understanding of their love for socializing after work. This all contributes to what makes Capetonians such happy and laid-back people.

50. WATCH THE SUN SET FROM THE MOUNTAIN

Sunsets in Cape Town are always incredible, but in summer there is something magical about them. At the end of each day, the sky is illuminated in pink and golden hues as if to thank the day for all it had shared.

One final bucket list item is to watch the sunset from a mountain. You can choose which one it will be. Hike or take the cableway up Table Mountain and watch the sun go down over the sea with Robben Island turning dark blue in the distance. Hike Lion's Head

>TOURIST

with a group of people and enjoy a bottle of wine at the top, watching as the clouds become outlined by liquid gold. Or for those who are not in the mood to do anything active, simply drive up to Signal Hill and open than bottle of wine on the side of the mountain, where there are sure to be other people enjoying the moment.

    Whichever spot you choose, Cape Town's sunset will stay with you for the rest of your life. Even the end of the day in this magical city is as hopeful and as beautiful as the beginning.

TOP REASONS TO BOOK THIS TRIP

- Natural beauty: There are few places in the world where you are so spoilt by natural beauty as in Cape Town. The Sea, the mountains, the animals and the plant life all come together to make a perfectly harmonious ecosystem.

- Food: The food scene is unique, innovative and big on quality.

- Wine: South African wines are celebrated around the world, and here you can taste award-winning cultivars for a fraction of the price you pay back home.

- The people: Capetonians are some of the friendliest people you will ever meet. Thanks to our country's melting pot of heritages, you will meet people you might never have considered speaking to, and find out that humanity and kind-heartedness was born in Cape Town.

>TOURIST

Greater Than a Tourist – Durban KwaZulu-Natal South Africa

50 Travel Tips from a Local

Nazeera Rawat

Copyright © 2017 CZYK Publishing

DEDICATION

This book is dedicated to my friends and family. For always giving me love and attention, no matter how much I needed! It is also dedicated to my cat, Salem, for coming home ALMOST every night during the past 12 years.

ABOUT THE AUTHOR

Nazeera Rawat is an avid photographer, cat lover and dreamer who lives Durban, South Africa. She has a Postgraduate degree in Psychology and loves to read, be creative and expand her horizons.

Nazeera loves to travel and is slowly ticking places off her very long list of must see places around the world. She loves to experience places from a non-conventional angle.

Nazeera likes to connect with people who are from the places she visits beforehand by utilizing the internet and joining online communities. It's the best way to experience the real love people have for their homes and enjoy all things local!

Nazeera is a born and bred Durbanite and knows how to have the best Durban experience! As they say in South Africa, Local is Lekker!

>TOURIST

My favourite part of travelling or having people visit me in my home town is getting the experience you wouldn't usually get otherwise. When you live in a place for a very long time you discover things you wouldn't by just spending a few weeks there.

Often a local doesn't even realise they are privy to so many amazing spots or restaurants because it can seem like just part of your everyday life! Little do they know a visitor would relish to be immersed in your local culture and local life, sometimes it's the little things that make the biggest impact on your memory of your holiday.

I love to make friends online so I end up with the opportunity to experience many different things in the countries I've visited over the years. The flipside of that is that when they visit me in South Africa I get to host them and show them why I LOVE Durban! The best part is that sometimes in accommodating a friend I learn new things about my city too!

Durban is a little, or not so little, beach town on the east coast of South Africa. We are very culturally diverse with the Indian culture and tradition having a strong impact on all the locals no matter their colour or religion! One thing I have learnt over the years is that we eat all our food really spicy! It surprised me to learn that a little bowl of crushed chili is NOT served at every restaurant around the world no matter your meal.

In Durban, and in South Africa generally, we are very into sport. It is common to see people out and about on normal days wearing supporters merchandise. The whole city tries to turn up for games and the atmosphere is really infectious!

Durban is known for being the friendliest city in South Africa so you will never have to worry about not having a good time here even if you choose to travel alone. Because of our laid back beach vibe it's the perfect place to take a relaxed holiday while still getting a sense of adventure! The term Local is Lekker, lekker meaning nice or good in Afrikaans, was coined as something to inspire pride in our nation, a sense of unity to truly show off our rainbow nation and all it has to offer.

Besides our easy going beachy vibes, Durban and surrounds also has strong historical value. One place being the site of one of the most significant points in our history, the Capture of Nelson Mandel which led to his 27 years of imprisonment!

Whether you're looking for the beach, history or both, fun and sun will greet you on your arrival!

1. BEST TIME TO VISIT

The best part about Durban is that it is ALWAYS a good time to visit. We have great weather all year around with hot summers and mild winters. An amazing selling point being the Indian Ocean! Guaranteeing warm water and fun in the sun no matter the time of year or season. 365 beach days a year anyone?

2. WHERE SHOULD I STAY?

Finding somewhere to stay in Durban is very easy. We have a coast lined with hotels end to end, both on the frontline (beach facing) and second row (no beach view). Besides the beach hotels there are many other hotels in the city and outlying areas. I personally prefer staying right on the beach. It is convenient and allows you to enjoy the sea air and view on those lazy days without leaving your room! There are also private apartments and houses by the beach that you can book with a little internet research.

3. GETTING AROUND

Getting around can become difficult if you don't know which types of transport to use. Ubers are popular but are not the only way to travel around the city. We do not have a good train service so your best bet would be vehicles. It's important to distinguish between a taxi and a cab, a cab is the type of transport you call when you need a ride somewhere, commonly called a taxi in other parts of the world. In South Africa a taxi is a very low cost form of transport most commonly used by the locals. You will easily recognize these as they tend to be 12 seater shuttle like vehicles. Another good way to get around the beach area and main city are buses called People Movers. These buses have regular stops and run long hours. Your most luxurious option would be to hire a car and drive around. This is a great option as parking is easy to find on the beach and is free! Just remember, here in South Africa we drive on the left!

4. EATING YOUR WAY THROUGH TOWN, EVEN ON A BUDGET!

Durbanites love to eat! There are countless places to eat no matter your budget or preferences. Durban has 2 signature dishes that are a must eat if visiting the city, Durban Curry and Bunny Chow! Don't be alarmed, no bunnies are harmed in the making of Bunny Chow, in fact it is a vegan dish. Other places to try include the Cargo Hold where you dine among Sharks at the Marine World Shark Tank,

Surf Riders Beach Café which serves vegan dishes and Haute Tea at the Oyster Box.

If you're looking for atmospheric nighttime dining then Florida Road is the perfect street to get your fix! If halal fast food or Indian Cuisine is what you crave then visit Sparks Road and you will be spoiled for choice. The most economical way of making sure you get all your meals AND save money is to visit a supermarket every few days and stock up on ingredients or foods that are easy to make and won't spoil.

5. SWING THE BIG RUSH BIG SWING – TALLEST IN THE WORLD!

Visit Durban's world famous Moses Mabhida Stadium to get a unique Durban experience. This is home to the tallest swing in the world. Climb up the side of the stadiums handle to a platform high above the field, strap in and then…jump off! It's a rush!

6. VIEW THE BEACH FROM ABOVE

While you're at the stadium make sure you ride the Sky Car to the viewing deck located at the apex of the 'basket handle'. This deck allows you to get amazing views of the coast from high above it all! Ride up and stay as long as you like, the car goes up and down every half hour.

>TOURIST

7. EXPERIENCE A 360° VIEW (WHILE REVOLVING!) OF DURBAN

Yes! You read right! Roma Revolving Restaurant is located on the Esplanade near the Durban Yacht Club. You can enjoy a lovely meal whilst getting an amazing view of Durban. As you revolve you will see the harbor, beach and inland toward the city and suburbs. Bookings are required and prices are average to high but it is well worth it! Don't worry if you are prone to motion sickness, I am too but you barely feel any movement.

As long as you don't pay too much attention to it, like staring at the floor where you can see the boundary between the revolving deck and stationary deck, you'll be completely fine. Don't forget your camera!

8. RIDE THE WAVES

A big attraction in Durban are the waves. Our beaches are a favourite spot for surfers and people who like to enjoy water sports. A day doesn't go by where you do not see surfers, jet skis, kayaks, yachts or windsurfers relishing the sun and warm Indian Ocean. There is a surfing club where you can get a few lessons before hitting the waves yourself but if that's not your style (it isn't mine either) I also enjoy sitting on the beach and watching the surfers or walking one of our many piers to get a closer look at the action!

9. SPEND THE WEEKEND EXPLORING USHAKA MARINE WORLD

Located at the southern end of Durban's coast line is Ushaka Marine World. There are quite a few things you can do here and it would probably take you a whole weekend if you wanted to do everything. The main attractions here are the Aquarium, Wet 'n Wild Water park and a small mall full of restaurants, surfing shops and African style souvenirs. You can also swim with the sharks or watch feedings, see a dolphin show or venture into the Dangerous Creatures Exhibit. There is enclosed pay parking on site if you prefer to take your own transport. Alternatively, Ushaka is a stop on the People Mover Bus Route.

10. DINE LIKE THE GODFATHER, AN OFFER YOU CAN'T REFUSE!

A unique experience is stopping for a bite at The Vapour Café. This café is themed after The Godfather movies and boasts a menu headed 'The Hit List' with meals named after characters from the movies. This café is perfect no matter the time of day, it always has a good vibe!

"Where ever you go, go with all your heart."

– Confucius

>TOURIST

11. BROWSE A MORNING MARKET

A favourite activity of mine as well as countless other Durbanites! Morning Markets are a huge thing here and so there are many to choose from. If you'd like a bite to eat after your early morning Sunday run (or just want food pronto) then a good place to stop at would be The Morning Trade, an organic and specialty food market. It has everything, from coconut water served in actual coconuts to gourmet cupcakes!

The only downside is that you have to be an early bird or you'll miss the worm (which I have done many times!). If you're looking for something more than just food then make sure to visit the iHeart Market located on the grounds of Moses Mabhida Stadium every first Saturday of the month. Here you will find food (of course) as well as handmade wares, upcoming designer clothes and vintage or antique items. It's the perfect place to find something one of a kind!

12. BUY HANDMADE PROUDLY SOUTH AFRICAN MERCHANDISE

Another place to buy something handmade is along the beach. Here there are countless local vendors who set up stalls and sell their wares. It's a great place to get an authentic handmade African souvenir. From experience I can tell you it's also a lifesaver in a beach related emergency such as breaking your flip flops or messing your shirt with ice cream!

13. RELEASE YOUR INNER CHILD AT FUNWORLD

Right on the beach is a small attraction that has fun rides, bumper cars and arcade games available for all ages. The ride people like most in this small theme park is the sky carriage, which takes you on a short ride high above the park! This is great for couples and kids love it to. A word of warning though: make sure to wear shoes that are firmly attached to your feet or they will fall off somewhere above the park and you will struggle to find them again!

14. STROLL WILSON'S WHARF

If you're looking for a low key outing or just want to start your day off nice and slow or relaxing then Wilson's Wharf is a good place to go. Built on the water and housing some restaurants and shops you can have a chilled out breakfast or lunch while breathing in the fresh sea air and enjoying the view. There are also a few activities you can book from ticket offices located here, like sea life tours, short cruises on the harbor or a morning on a yacht out at sea.

15. WAKE UP EARLY TO WATCH THE SUNRISE!

The best thing about this tip is that it's free and AMAZING. Have you ever seen a sunrise? Now have you ever seen the sun rise over the Indian Ocean slowly lighting up the beach, the awakening of the birds, the waves dotted with early morning surfers? This is something I love and never get tired of doing. As someone who has spent their whole life in Durban, I'm still excited to see a sunrise like this every time. No matter how many times I've seen it, I always want to see it again!

>TOURIST

16. HIKE A NATURE TRAIL

This is also something you can do for free depending on your level of confidence hiking. There are trails that anyone can just hike or you can go with a guide on a guided hike. Hikes are readily available almost everywhere in Durban and the surrounding areas. It's a city lush with vegetation, rivers and protected areas which are perfect for hiking!

17. VISIT HOWICK FALLS AND GET A WAFFLE ON A STICK

Howick Falls is our very own little waterfall a couple of hours drive out of Durban. Here you can hike, walk under the falls or swim. If you leave early and don't mind returning after dark then this activity is easily done in one day. Don't forget to stop at a vendor that sells delicious waffles on a stick with a variety of toppings and dips, a sweet treat after your hike.

18. EXPERIENCE A BIT OF HISTORY AT THE MANDELA CAPTURE SITE

Also a couple of hours drive out of Durban, this little slice of earth marks a very important day and place in South African history. The exact location of the road block that led to Nelson Mandela's arrest and subsequent 27 years of imprisonment. It is marked by an artistic installation, a monument celebrating our great leader, and is accompanied by a small museum.

Even if you are not a history buff the artist designed his installation in a very creative way. If you stand in one exact spot the metal spires converge to form the iconic picture of Mr Mandela's face.

19. TAKE A VINTAGE TRAIN THROUGH THE VALLEY OF 1000 HILLS

One of the last operating steam engine trains takes you on a scenic ride through the Midlands Meander and Valley of 1000 Hills. With spectacular views and a 1 hour stop to picnic this is an amazing family outing for children of all ages and even adults! Ever wanted to ride the Hogwarts Express? Here's your chance! There are also souvenir shops, some food stalls and bathroom facilities at the stop.

20. DRINK COFFEE AS FRESH AS IT GETS!

A short drive out of the city and you hit an area called Assagay. This is an area known for its farms, in particular, coffee bean farms! You will have to book in advance for a tour of any one of the many coffee bean farms available. On the tour they will take you through the whole process of coffee making, from growing the plants to bottling the coffee you find on your table! The tour usually ends with a sampling of fresh coffee in various strengths. You can also buy bags of coffee and other homemade products such as coffee soaps and coffee flavoured fudge.

>TOURIST

"We shall not cease from exploration, and the end of all our loring will be to arrive where we started and know the place for the first time."

– T.S Elliot

21. SADDLE UP AND EXPLORE THE MIDLAND MEANDER

Go horseback riding through the Midlands Meander. This is a very scenic and beautiful area that has a river and some wildlife that you could spot on your ride. Be one with nature and take in the fresh air and sun while not having to do much work yourself! If you prefer not to take a horse out you can still take short rides within estates. Make it a family affair too!

22. BIKE THE GOLDEN MILE

It is very common to see people biking up and down our paved coast line from North to South or vice versa, we call this the Golden Mile. It is lined with hotels and restaurants and paved all the way down both sides.

The promenade is always full of people skateboarding, rollerblading or just plain walking and running. What people don't realise is that you can hire bikes hourly at either side if you don't own your own bike! You can even go a little further and join up at Moses Mabhida Stadium.

23. SHOP TILL YOU DROP AT GATEWAY: THEATRE OF SHOPPING

Gateway is the biggest mall we have to offer in Durban. It's about 20 minutes from the beachfront. Besides the usual shops and restaurants, this mall has some unique features. One is that there is a theatre inside the mall that regularly puts on plays, shows and concerts.

Another is an indoor wave simulator. This is quite popular with the locals and visitors alike and it always packed with people. If you need to practice your surfing skills or just find the open ocean a bit scary then this is perfect for you! Other features include indoor rock climbing, rooftop go-carting and a 5D cinema.

24. GET IN THE SPORTING SPIRIT

South Africans are avid supporters of our sports teams and really get into the spirit of 'backing our boys'. Durban is the home of the Sharks rugby team, a very successful South African team! We have dedicated stadiums for soccer, rugby and cricket in Durban so there is always some kind of event or match taking place.

Experiencing a South African sports match is a great way to get a feel of our nation and culture. We regularly host our national teams, the Springboks and the Proteas, as well as international teams. I always enjoy the atmosphere and love that surrounds the crowd as we wear green and gold and cheer on our teams!

>TOURIST

25. SPOT THE BIG 5 ON SAFARI FEATURING AN AFRICAN SUNSET!

An absolute must do when visiting South Africa is to go on a Safari! Here in Durban and surrounding areas there are many Game Drives and Safaris you can go on so take your pick. You can easily spot our Big 5 all year around. I recommend taking an evening Safari to get a chance to witness that movie-scene-like African Sunset! It's a beautiful sight to behold.

26. GET YOUR HANDS DIRTY ON THE SARDINE RUN

A famous phenomenon that takes place on Durbans coast once a year is the Sardine Run. This is a time when 1000's of sardines migrate across our coast. 1000's of people flock to the beach to watch them swim past like a huge wave, flopping and splashing out of the water. People also use this time to do a little fishing!

27. APPRECIATE SOME OF THE BEST AND FUNNIEST SAND ART AROUND

It is common to find areas of the beach cordoned off for sand art as you walk along our beach. These sand artists are very talented, often creating interactive art such as couches to sit in, fine dining settings or convertible sports cars. You can have your picture taken with the exhibits for a fantastic holiday memory. Sometimes the artists take to showing off their political views with funny portrayals of South African current affairs! It's always a fun stop in your day.

28. TAKE A RICKSHAW RIDE, YOU WON'T REGRET IT

You may notice colourful 2 seater benches on 2 wheels being pulled by a colourful and happy looking man or woman, these are called rickshaws! This is a fun and quick activity to experience a little slice of our tribal culture. A ride can be as long or short as you want with prices differing according to the length.

29. CRUISE THE INDIAN OCEAN

Durban offers a number of cruises that leave right from our harbor. The best part is that you can choose any amount of days you want! From 2 day weekend cruises to 9 day cruises, you choose your stay even if you're tight on time. A very popular cruise is the 3 day Portuguese Island cruise. This cruise takes you just off the coast of Mozambique to scarcely inhabited Islands where you can spend the day tanning or experiencing the local tribe culture. You can also choose to stay on the ship and enjoy one of the many activities available to you onboard.

30. RENT OUT A HOUSE AT ZIMBALI

A short 25 minute drive out of Durban is the Zimbali Game Reserve. This is a protected area which offers a 5 star hotel and full golf course on its grounds. Personally I prefer renting out one of the many private lodges that are located around the reserve, you can rent these out for varying amounts of time. From here you can hike down to the beach, golf or go animal spotting. There are strict rules that have to be followed within the Reserve and these rules are strictly enforced. It is common to spot deer or zebra grazing around within arms distance!

>TOURIST

"Many a trip continues long after movement in time and space have ceased."

– John Steinbeck

31. HIT A HOLE IN ONE!

Durban is also big on golfing. There about 4 golf courses dotted around the city with a few more within an hour's drive. If golfing is your thing Durban is definitely the place to make your mark! If you prefer mini golf we have that too, both indoor and outdoor courses.

32. SPEND A NIGHT AT THE RACES

Night racing is an exciting event here in Durban with many people making an evening out of it. Greyville Racecourse often holds night time racing as part of their regular schedule. Whether or not you would like to bet on the race, attending a night race is an amazing and exciting experience!

33. CATCH A FISH, THERE ARE PLENTY!

A very common pastime in Durban is, of course, fishing! You will routinely spot fisherman in the early hours of the morning and all through the day set up their poles at the end of the piers at the best fishing spots. Most of these fisherman are locals fishing for fun so feel free to ask them to let you have a go! Most often any fish caught are let back into the ocean and not harmed.

34. WANDER THE ART DISTRICT

The art district in Durban is fairly small but very interesting to drive around in or walk through. There are many art galleries you can visit but there is also a magnitude of street art, graffiti and installations to tickle your fancy. The art district is also dotted with unique artisan cafes, restaurants and shops. Well worth spending an afternoon exploring!

35. ATTEND AN EXPO

One thing Durban has no shortage of are Expos! The Durban Exhibition Centre hosts many expos scattered across the whole year. Some of these include the House and Garden Show, the Food and Wine show, Top Gear and many souks and fairs including The Eastern Bridal Fair. We even host a Sexpo once a year! If you are interested in one find out when it is running and stop by. Shows usually run for 5-10 days and basic entrance tickets are usually cheap!

36. BOOK A WEEKEND AT THE DRAKENSBURG MOUNTAINS

The Drakensburg Mountains make a great family weekend getaway. It is a few hours' drive out of Durban but it is worth the drive! Here you can hike, enjoy springs, mountain climbing and basically any outdoor sport or activity you can think of. The Drakensberg Mountains are a world heritage site and therefore is also a protected area. This means you can enjoy getting up close and personal with nature and the wildlife! It is common for it to snow here during winter and temperatures do drop quite low so don't forget to bundle up a bit if you're visiting during the winter months.

>TOURIST

37. EXPLORE DURBAN'S HISTORICAL SITES, ARCHITECTURE AND MUSEUMS

Durban is home to many historical sites, amazing architecture dating back to colonial times and some really cool Military and Maritime Museums. Our city center features beautiful buildings including the main post office building, City Hall and The British Museum. We also have a Holocaust Museum situated near the beach front. If you don't mind creepy vibes you can also explore abandoned prisons and hospitals!

38. FEEL LIKE A GIANT AS YOU WALK MINI TOWN!

An activity that always attracts a lot of people is a small place (literally) called Mini Town! Located on the beachfront, this place allows you to walk the whole of Durban in just a few short minutes. The miniaturised city is great for people of all ages and features all major landmarks and building in Durban. It's also a great place for photo ops!

39. TWEET SURROUNDED BY 100'S OF SPECIES OF BIRDS

If you are a bird enthusiast then The Umgeni Bird Park should definitely be on your list of things to do in Durban. With 100's of species of birds to admire it is sure to keep you occupied for hours. Tickets are available at the door and there is parking available on site. Beware! The toucans bite! Make sure to keep your fingers outside the wire mesh at all times because I can vouch that getting your finger bitten is not pleasant!

40. PICNIC AT MITCHELL PARK

Mitchell Park is a favourite destination for weekend outings and picnics. It is located very near to Florida Road as well where you can get food. The park is large, very shady and provides tables and benches if you prefer not to sit on the ground. There is a children's play area with swings and such. A nice feature is the presence of a small zoo on site. This zoo has quite a variety of animals and makes a fun addition to your day.

> *"Not all those who wander are lost."*
> – J.R.R. Tolkien

41. ROCK OUT TO LOCAL MUSIC EVERY SUNDAY AT BOTANICAL GARDENS

This is an activity much loved by the locals and it is easy to see why! Every Sunday afternoon at the Durban Botanical Gardens there is an outdoor concert near the lake called Music at the Lake. South African artists both nationally and internationally famous as well as newcomers perform here every week. Sometimes even international artists perform! Tickets are cheap but there are a limited number available. Make sure you bring something to eat and a blanket to sit on as the vibe is usually pretty chilled out.

42. GLAM UP FOR THE DURBAN JULY EVENT!

The Durban July is an event many South Africans wait all year for. It is attended by people across South Africa who flock to Durban during this time. The event is known for showcasing unique and eccentric designer wear. Tickets can be expensive but includes entrance to the event and horse racing on the day. If the fancy vibe isn't your thing there are many after-parties you can attend, arguably what people are really waiting for!

43. HOP ON THE DURBAN CITY OPEN TOP BUS TOUR

I recently got to host a friend from Switzerland but all she had time for was just one full day here in Durban. I spent some time pondering the best way to get her to see the whole city in a limited amount of time and decided on this bus tour. It was great! We got to see the whole city in just a few hours and it was cheap! There is a little bit of commentary but it's very basic. The tour leaves from the beachfront twice a day every day.

44. SOAK UP PANORAMIC VIEWS FROM THE CUBE LOOKOUT

This spot is amazing to get views of the beach and Moses Mabhida stadium. It's got a monument on the side called The Cube but the real attraction is the view. The spot isn't on any public transport routes so you may have to take a cab but it is worth it!

45. JOIN AN ASTROTURF SOCCER MATCH

This is something that usually happens spur of the moment but it's a ton of fun! Durban is dotted with countless Astroturf courts. Boys and girls of all ages book these hourly to play mini games of soccer or mini tournaments. Such is life that often a team is one or two players short, sometimes people drop out or get injured. That's your chance! Teams will look for people to join them, often inviting whoever is walking by or hanging out at the courts. It's a great atmosphere and experience.

46. TREAT YOURSELF TO A SPA DAY AT CAMP ORCHIDS

Camp Orchids is an estate located about 20 minutes outside of Durban. It includes a wedding venue, some activities and a spa. The estate also stables horses. The reason I love the spa there is because its serene and peaceful and you are surrounded by beautiful grounds. It really is the perfect environment to relax and enjoy pampering yourself!

47. ZIP-LINE ACROSS ORIBI GORGE

If I had to recommend one adventure as a MUST do it would be zip-lining across Oribi Gorge! I will admit it is scary at first and I almost didn't do it but I'm glad I did it in the end. I would have regretted it if I didn't! there are 2 options here, you can take the single zip-line which is a shortcut and takes you along the gorge or you can do the full 14 line zip course. I recommend doing the full 14! The first half will get you right to the edge of the gorge and then you zip across! The other half gets you back down. It's an amazing experience with amazing views, though it does take some strength as you are responsible for slowing yourself down. I did it in the rain so they operate in almost all weather conditions. You can also hike up to the rope bridge and walk across the gorge to a viewing deck. Not for people afraid of heights!

48. EXPLORE CASTLE ON MAIN

I found this gem by accident one day. I was driving the outskirts of Durban and saw a castle like building nestled on the side of the road. I turned in and noticed a café and some quaint little shops. I decided to go in and grab a coffee and ended up chatting to the server who mentioned that the upstairs was unfinished and has been abandoned for quite some time. The best news being that if I wanted to explore I was welcome to! It was a little creepy to climb up but I really enjoyed the experience. As an avid photographer it was like gold to me! The café downstairs has an amazing vegetarian and vegan menu which you should check out whether you want to explore the castle or not.

49. LIGHT UP YOUR LIFE AT THE UMHLANGA LIGHTHOUSE

About 25 minutes out of Durban you will find our restored but unused lighthouse. It's a popular spot for locals as there are many restaurants around the area. You are able to walk right up to the lighthouse and the beach is just beyond it. It's one of the prettiest places you could visit!

50. WATER SPORT TO YOUR HEARTS CONTENT

Dams, dams and more dams! Durbanites LOVE to utilize their dams to the fullest. There is not a day when the water is free of boats, jet skis, canoes and many other things! You will be hard pressed to find a water activity you cannot do at the dam.

They even have ab-sailing and zip-lines that end mid dam making you have to let go! Many activities are available for a fee, many are free and many only require you to hire the equipment. All that aside, it's easy to make friends and get invited to tag along. Many families own boats and other water equipment and are only too happy to have you along. The more the merrier!

Top Reasons to Book This Trip

- Beaches: Some of the best beaches in the world.
- Food: Amazing fusion of foods unique to South Africa.
- Rainbow Nation: A rich heritage of tradition and culture all under one nation.
- Weather: Beautiful weather all year around!
- People: The best and most friendly people you will ever meet!
- Value for money: Definitely a place you can get the most out of your trip!
- Great for a family holiday: There is something for everyone! Whether you want to be active, relax, explore, eat or play.

>TOURIST

GREATER THAN A TOURIST – JOHANNESBURG GAUTENG SOUTH AFRICA

50 Travel Tips from a Local

Micheline Logan

DEDICATION

This book is dedicated to my friend Fabienne, who refuses to let cancer get the better of her. Wishing her many more years.

ABOUT THE AUTHOR

Micheline is a silver surfer who lives in Johannesburg. She loves the outdoors and wildlife, especially birdwatching, which makes South Africa a great place to live.

Micheline is widely travelled: Her father was in the Royal Airforce, and by the time she was eight, she had crossed the equator by sea three times. She has travelled to South America, the US, Europe, the Middle East, Australia and Asia, and, of course in Africa.

One of her other interests is open-water swimming, which has taken her to the Greek Islands, Turkey and the Red Sea.

While she loves to experience the world, she is always happy to come home to Johannesburg, where she lives and works. One thing about Jozi - it's never boring!

>TOURIST

Many tourists to South Africa land at O R Tambo Airport near Johannesburg en route to other destinations such as Cape Town, Durban or the Kruger National Park. Joburg (as we know it) is perceived as a commercial capital where people go to do business and little else. This is a pity, because Joburg, Jozi or Egoli has so much to offer. Although Joburg is less than 200 years old, our ancestors have been living in its vicinity since man started walking on two legs - their past is still being unearthed. We made some wrong turns along the way, and the legacy of apartheid is recorded for you to see as well. If you are a daredevil, you can bungee-jump off a cooling tower; if you like shopping you can visit our markets, unless you are into shopping malls, of which there are plenty.

Maybe you do not have the time to visit one of our major game reserves; don't worry, we have nature reserves in and around Johannesburg that will give you a taste of Africa (and bring you back again).

There is no particular order to the tips here, except that I start off with rather laid-back places to visit and stroll around. While you won't get altitude sickness in Joburg, the thin air may make you quite tired for a day or two, so take it easy in the beginning, by visiting one or two of our open spaces to acclimatize.

You could spend a year in Joburg and not get to see and do everything, I have included some of my favourites here, but there are other attractions. The challenge is not what to experience, it is what to miss out on. Hopefully you will return again and again!

1. SOME INTERESTING FACTS ABOUT JOBURG

Johannesburg is also known as Joburg (which is a branded name for the city), Jozi, and Egoli. Egoli means "City of Gold", referring to Joburg's early days as a mining camp.

Johannesburg's altitude is almost 1800 metres above sea level. Water boils at 98_oC. By the way, Joburg tap water is safe to drink.

Johannesburg is the world's largest landlocked city - it does not have a major river or lake and is hundreds of kilometres from the sea. Strangely enough, despite the lack of water, it is a port city - the largest inland port in Africa.

Although there are no major rivers, two streams are found on either side of the Witwatersrand, a rocky ridge just north of the city centre and the continental watershed. All the rain that falls south of the ridge flows into the Atlantic via the Vaal and Orange River; the rain that falls north of the ridge flows via the Limpopo into the Indian Ocean.

What it lacks in water, Joburg makes up for in trees. There are an estimated 10 million trees planted in Joburg, making it one of the world's largest man-made urban forests.

2. GETTING AROUND JOBURG

Johannesburg is a large and sprawling metropolis and, while there is public transport, it is easiest to get around either by self-drive with a hire car and a GPS or using a taxi. South African cars are right-hand-drive and the roads are generally good, but you need to be quite an assertive driver to cope with the local drivers, especially minibus taxis. Fuel is quite expensive, and like most cities, rush hour is to be avoided (6am-8am and 4pm-6:30pm).

Like most cities, Uber is alive and well and at your bid and call. If you are pressed for time, there is a tourist bus that has a selection of routes that gives you lots of bang for your buck.

3. NOT MUCH TIME? TAKE A BUS

If you are pressed for time and have only a day or two to spend sightseeing, the City Bus Sightseeing tours are a great option. These tours, done in either an open-top double-decker, or a 16 seater minibus, are an ideal way to see Joburg and many of the sights mentioned here. The bus logo indicates if an attraction is on the bus route. You buy a ticket for the route and can hop off and on at any of the destinations en route. There is a city route, that includes Constitutional Hill and Gold Reef City, a route that takes you through some of Joburg's suburbs, and a Soweto route, which can be combined with the city route.

4. THOSE TEN MILLION TREES

Stand on a high point in Johannesburg, like Northcliff or Parktown and you will see greenery stretching out everywhere. Johannesburg is actually a grassland biome with few trees, but a tradition of planting trees by early settlers has continued to this day. One of the early attempts was Sachsenwald Forest, planted by Hermann Eckstein at the turn of the nineteenth century as a timber plantation. The name was later anglicised to Saxonwold, one of the upmarket suburbs of modern-day Johannesburg.

If you visit in October, you will be treated to the sight of thousands of Jacarandas in bloom. This Brazilian import cloaks the city in mauve, and is a Japanese tourist attraction. Many Japanese visit Johannesburg and Pretoria at this time and wear clothes that match the marvellous blossoms. Exams fall soon after October, and there is a superstition that you will pass your exams if a blossom falls on you.

5. THE ZOO AND ZOO LAKE

On the border of Saxonwold lies the Johannesburg Zoo and the Zoo Lake. This land was also part of Hermann Eckstein's farm Braamfontein. After his death, in 1903, his business partners bequeathed 200 acres to Johannesburg for the recreational use of everyone who lived in Johannesburg. A small zoo was started, with the first animals being donated by Sir Percy Fitzpatrick (most famous for his book "Jock of the Bushveld" about his beloved dog). An artificial lake was constructed soon afterwards, and to this day, people of all colours and creeds enjoy walking, picknicking and boating around the Lake.

The Zoo is large (140 acres) and has some rare animals such as white lion, bongo antelope and Lord Derby Eland. Both the zoo and the Zoo lake are very busy on weekends, but fairly quiet during the week.

6. EMMARENTIA AND LOUW GELDENHUYS

Joburg was an interesting mix of gold mining and farms. Like Hermann Eckstein who was both a mining magnate and a farmer, the Geldenhuys family had a large farm and also prospected for gold. These were exciting times - between 1885 and 1895, the population of Joburg grew from 2 000 to 100 000 because of the gold rush.

Following the Anglo-Boer War, when many able men were out of work, Louw Geldenhuys commissioned the Emmarentia Dam (named after his wife). This dam provided irrigation for farms which he parcelled out and is another favourite recreation spot for Joburgers, although it is now surrounded by suburbs. If you drive along Greenfield road, you can still see Louw Geldenhuys' farmhouse, which is a beautifully maintained and privately owned heritage building. It typically has a "stoep" (verandah) around the building and there are impressive palms in the garden. A few hundred metres further on is Marks Park Sports and recreation centre, where his brother Frans' house is now the clubhouse.

Emmarentia Dam has a botanical garden adjacent to it, as well as a park where dog lovers can let their dogs run free and have a great time. At the top of the Emmarentia Ridge is Melville Koppies, which can be visited on the weekends and holds more clues to Joburg's past.

7. MELVILLE KOPPIES

Melville Koppies (hills) lies just across the road from Marks Park, and people have been living there for at least the last 250 000 years. The original inhabitants were stone age men and Khoisan people who were probably displaced by Iron Age nomadic Setswana, based on remains of iron smelting pits found on the koppies.

The rise of the Zulu nation created great disruptions in the 1820s and the inhabitants of Melville Koppies and other communities were in turn displaced by the turmoil.

Wits University runs educational walks, both about the history and the fauna and flora of the koppies on weekends, which is when the public have access to this spot. From the top of the ridge, you can get a great view of Johannesburg and what was the original Braamfontein farm.

8. KLIPRIVIERSBERG NATURE RESERVE

Want to see wildlife but you don't have enough time to get to any of our great game reserves? Klipriviersberg is just a few kilometres from the city centre where you can get a first-hand experience of the South African veld and maybe see some antelope and zebra.

People have lived in these valleys long before Joburg came to be. Daily entrance to the reserve is free, with occasional organised walks, which you can join for a small fee, which goes towards maintaining the reserve. They usually include a slap-up breakfast.

You can spend a whole day traversing the many trails in the Reserve. Some are on level ground, others are quite challenging. Apart from wildlife such as blesbok or wildebeest, there is good birding, with lovely birds like white-fronted bee-eaters. Take your binoculars!

The main entrance is in Peggy Vera Road in Kibler Park, with secure parking.

9. TAKE A WALK ON THE WILDS SIDE

The Randlords were a group of personalities and founders of mining companies in the early days of Joburg. While they lived in great luxury in their magnificent mansions, some of which can still be seen, they also were mindful of the citizens of Johannesburg. Like Hermann Eckstein, the colourful Barney Barnato left open parkland to be used in perpetuity by the people of Joburg. Dating from 1925, the Wilds are copiously forested and many specimens of indigenous plants grow here. The Park became unsafe about twenty years ago, and people stopped visiting, but it now has a renaissance. Artist James Delaney, who lives near the Wilds has installed an Owl Garden with over 60 owl statues. People started coming back and it is becoming a popular venue again.

10. FEELING PECKISH? NEIGHBOURGOODS

Every Saturday, the commercial suburb of Braamfontein hosts Neighbourgoods, a food market with cuisines to satisfy every palate. Artisanal breads, handcrafted beers and food from all over the world (don't miss the paella!).

On the rooftop there is live entertainment and a few bars.

There are also some craft stalls which might just have those gifts you want to take back home.

Parking can be an issue, so you can take an Uber, or visit via a hop-on hop-off City sightseeing bus.

Neighbourgoods is open from 09:00 - 15:00.

"All roads lead to Johannesburg"

Alan Paton, author of "Cry the Beloved Country"

11. ORIGINS CENTRE MUSEUM

Also situated in Braamfontein is the Origins Centre Museum of Witwatersrand University, less than 2 kilometres from Neighbourgoods and open from Monday to Saturday. This fascinating museum explores our earliest beginnings and has an extensive collection of early tools and rock art.

There is also comprehensive information about the San (Bushman) tribes and their culture, from which we could take some lessons in how to live and share.

Well worth a visit for a couple of hours. If you are feeling adventurous, you can get your DNA tested here.

12. HAVE YOUR DNA ANALYSED

You can get your DNA tested at the Origins Museum, usually on the first Saturday of each month. You will need to book in advance, as the event is limited to 60 guests. Presentations about evolution and genetic ancestry are given, and you can either just sign up for the talks or opt for DNA testing as well. The test results take about 8-14 weeks to be completed (the quick turnaround on DNA testing you see on TV is strictly fiction) and can be posted to you on completion. Please refer to the Origins Museum website for pricing and to download the application form.

13. THE CRADLE OF MANKIND – MAROPENG

If you enjoyed Origins, you must not miss Maropeng in the "Cradle of Humankind". This World Heritage site north-west of Johannesburg is famous for the number of remains of very early hominids found in the various caves in the region, like "Mrs Ples" and "Little Foot". Over 40% of the world's hominid fossils have been found here, truly justifying the name of "Cradle of Humankind".

Maropeng is a museum built to house some of these finds and depicts the history of our earliest forefathers. The museum is built in the form of a tumulus (burial mound) and starts our story with the first emergence of life on our planet.

You can combine this with a visit to one of the caves where these archaeological finds have been made, if you are not claustrophobic, the Sterkfontein Caves.

14. STERKFONTEIN CAVES

This is where many of the remains displayed at Maropeng were discovered. The Sterkfontein Caves have been open for viewing for nearly 100 years. The presence of fossils was first noted by miners in the 1890s. They were mining the caves for limestone. Raymond Dart and Robert Broom started an archaeological dig in the 1930s with their students from the University of the Witwatersrand, which is still in progress today.

While the mining probably destroyed hundreds of fossils, about 500 hominids have been identified, as well as many mammals, some of which are extinct today.

The caves are quite cool as you walk through them. Some openings are a bit narrow, but it is an exhilarating trip to combine with Maropeng.

15. GILROY'S PUB AND RESTAURANT

While there are quite a few venues where you can have a meal in the vicinity of Maropeng, Gilroy's Pub offers some light entertainment after your educational visits. Wooden benches and tables are set around a roomy courtyard where reasonably priced and tasty pub grub is served, such as fish and chips, pies, and other hearty fare. There are salads and some fusion food too, which you can accompany with one of Gilroy's craft beers.

On the weekends there will be one or more artists singing for their supper, usually with a folk/Irish flavour. A great place to relax for all ages. There are also a few shops selling goodies such as handmade soaps, African curios and other items to add to your luggage.

16. CARNIVORE RESTAURANT

You may have heard of the original Carnivore restaurant in Nairobi. This is the South African franchise, where you can eat conventional dishes, both carnivorous and vegetarian, or you can opt to eat some flesh you have not tried before, like crocodile, ostrich and other African game. You can eat as much as you like, and admit defeat by lowering the flag on your table; until you do this, the waiters will bring you more and more to eat.

There is also a kiddies' menu available. The meat is cooked on an open fire, you might call it a barbecue; we South Africans call it a braai or braaivleis, literally "roasted meat".

17. NIROX PARK

Based in the area of the Cradle of Humankind, Nirox park is a 15-hectare artists' park, with sculptures strategically placed in the gardens. Some of the artists reside and work in the park.

The park is open from 10-17:00 on weekends to the public. A private visit can be arranged by contacting Nirox, where you can visit the artist's studios by previous arrangement.

Occasional events and concerts are held, notably a festival in winter, when various eating establishments from the Cape come and set up pop-up food stalls. This is a very popular event and tickets have to be booked well in advance.

With abundant ponds and dams, Nirox is a tranquil haven to visit and relax.

18. WALTER SISULU BOTANICAL GARDENS

On the West Rand, these beautiful botanical gardens are a great place to chill, attend the occasional concert or look for the famous black eagles that nest on the cliff over the waterfall (There is another pair near Klipriviersberg, but they are not so easy to see). You can bring your own picnic or buy food at the tea-room and restaurant.

These gardens were officially opened in the 1980s, but have been enjoyed by generations before then. There is a bird hide adjoining a small dam and special botanical sections for cycads, ferns, aloes, ethnobotanical plants and other examples of South Africa's floral kingdoms.

19. MONTECASINO BIRD GARDENS

While Montecasino is a casino in the North of Johannesburg, it also has other attractions, such as the Bird Gardens. This is a pleasant spot with walk-through aviaries housing local and exotic bird species. In addition, there is a show held 2-3 times a day, where birds interact with their keepers and the audience. The birds perform "acts", based on their natural behaviour, such as a crow that picks up tin cans. It can be quite impressive having a Eurasian Eagle Owl or a White-backed Vulture flying just over your head when you are sitting in the small ampitheatre!

In addition to birds, there are a few mammals, such as lemurs and meerkats, reptile exhibits and a small collection of frogs and spiders. There is also a pleasant tea-room called the Flamingo, where you can relax.

20. IL TEATRO AT MONTECASINO

The Theatre at Montecasino can stage large-scale events and has hosted fabulous shows like the "Lion King" and "West Side Story". The quality and energy of these shows is world-class.

Check up if there are any shows on that take your fancy.

There are many places to eat inside the casino and theatre complex, including fish restaurants and Italian. There are venues for the whole family, apart from the Bird garden, such as a bowling alley, movies and a kid's entertainment section. There is even a creche.

> *"I learnt during all those years to love Johannesburg, even though it was a mining camp. It was in Johannesburg that I found my most precious friends. It was in Johannesburg that the foundation for the great struggle of Passive Resistance was laid… Johannesburg, therefore had the holiest of all the holy association that Mrs Gandhi and I will carry back to India"*
>
> – Mohandas Gandhi, 1914

21. MAHATMA GANDHI AND JOHANNESBURG

Many South Africans are unaware what a major part South Africa, and Johannesburg, played in the Mahatma's life. There is a museum at Satyagraha House in Orchards.

This is where Gandhi formulated the concept of passive resistance or "satyagraha" when he stayed here in 1908-9 with his close friend, Hermann Kallenbach, an architect, who designed the house.

You can also stay at Satyagraha House, but it is not budget accommodation.

There are other sites in Johannesburg that commemorate Gandhi and there is a specialist tour that can take you round to all the places, if you wish. When you visit Constitution Hill, you will be reminded that Gandhi was imprisoned there, like so many other important figures of South African history.

22. CONSTITUTION HILL

This is one of the must-sees of your trip. Formerly a fort during the Anglo-Boer war and a notorious prison, this building on Braamfontein's ridge is now the site of South Africa's Constitutional Court, where disputes around constitutional matters are judged.

While thousands of prisoners spent their time here, we remember Mahatma Gandhi, Nelson Mandela, Albert Luthuli, Robert Sobukwe, Winnie Mandela, Albertina Sisulu and Fatima Meer as some of the inmates. The prisons they were held in can be visited.

There is also a comprehensive art collection that started on a shoestring budget and expanded dramatically, including woks from renowned artists such as Marc Chagall and William Kentridge.

23. LILIESLEAF FARM

Liliesleaf Farm in Rivonia was a sanctuary for the South African Communist party and the liberation movement and most of the key figures stayed or met here, including Nelson Mandela and Walter Sisulu.

Visitors to the heritage site can watch an audiovisual presentation of the history and times of the place and the people and see museum exhibits. The proceedings of the Rivonia trial were based on the people who were arrested at Liliesleaf.

24. APARTHEID MUSEUM

A must-visit experience to try and understand the lunacy that was apartheid. The architectural design was inspired by the content and has many symbols integrated into the building.

When you visit the museum, it is an experimental pilgrimage that enables you to understand what life was like living under apartheid if your skin was not white. The classifications were arbitrary: Chinese were regarded as "black", while Japanese were "honorary whites" because of the trade South Africa did with Japan.

Children under 12 are not admitted to the museum because of the graphic imagery contained there.

25. GOLD REEF CITY

You might think it odd to write about the Apartheid Museum and then about a casino and theme park, but the fact of the matter is that the Apartheid Museum is right next door to Gold Reef City, and it was built by the Casino consortium as a contribution to society.

While it is a theme park and has fun rides, Gold Reef City is built over an actual mine and one can experience some of the mining experience; taking the lift down to a mining stope, watching gold being poured and panning for gold.

Apart from the gold mining history and the fun rides, there is even a Victorian chapel that was originally built for the miners of Joburg. This chapel has been moved, brick by brick to the current site and can be used as a wedding venue.

26. CITY BUS TOUR TO SOWETO

There are many sights to see in Soweto (this exotic name is actually an abbreviation of South-West Township) and the best way to experience them is via a guided tour or the City Bus Sightseeing Soweto extension, which can be combined with the Red Bus tour. The starting point for the tour is at the Apartheid museum, where the Red Bus tour will drop you off. Alternatively you can arrange one of the many guided tours through your hotel or other accommodation.

There are also biking tours for the more athletically inclined.

You should visit the main tourist spots, as well as stop at some of the famous eateries, such as Sakhumzi's en route, starting with the FNB Stadium

27. FNB STADIUM (SOCCER CITY)

When South Africa won the opportunity to host the Fifa Soccer World Cup in 2010, although there were stadiums in the main cities and towns, many of them needed revamping to cater for the huge crowds that would fill them. Soccer city (now known as the FNB Stadium) was rebuilt in the form of a giant calabash and is the largest stadium in Africa.

You can take a guided tour of the stadium, or even better, you can attend a soccer match or even a concert if the timing is right. Performers as diverse as Santana and Lady Gaga have performed here.

>TOURIST

28. VILAKAZI STREET

Famous for being the only street on the planet where two Nobel laureates lived, Vilakazi Street is now lined with places to eat and shop. The two laureates are Nelson Mandela and Desmond Tutu, who still shares his time between his home in Cape Town and his simple house on Vilakazi Street.

Mandela's house is now a small museum, which takes about 15 minutes to see.

You can browse the shops for local handcrafts and try some township cuisine at Sakhumzi or one of the other spots after visiting the museum. There is also a container shop called the Box Shop which contains a roastery called Kofi and a design store.

29. BUNGEE JUMP OFF A COOLING TOWER

For the daredevil in you, here is an opportunity to bungee jump under controlled conditions. The jump takes place between the two vibrantly painted towers.

You do not have to bungee off these cooling towers, the remnants of an old power station, you can just get to the top and have a great view. There is a Chisanyama (grilled meat) restaurant at the base of the towers. If you take one of the Soweto bicycle tours or the bus tour, the cooling towers are part of the route.

30. HECTOR PIETERSON MEMORIAL

Hector Pieterson was a 12-year old who was shot dead by a policeman in the June 1976 Soweto Uprising. Children from Soweto took to the streets to protest against learning Afrikaans at school. Hector was one of the first casualties.

Two blocks from the memorial there is a museum dedicated to him and those dark times. It explains the problems of the segregated education of the time, and why the children protested. The reaction of the police that day was totally out of proportion and brutal.

> *"No one is born hating another person because of the colour of his skin, or his background, or his religion. People must learn to hate, and if they can learn to hate, they can be taught to love, for love comes more naturally to the human heart than its opposite."*
>
> - Nelson Mandela - Long Walk to Freedom.

31. WORLD OF BEER

The Newtown Precinct, which can be accessed via the City Bus sightseeing red Route, is one of the oldest parts of Joburg and has many attractions for a day tour.

The World of Beer is a museum to the world's oldest brew, and was established by South African Breweries, which became SAB-Miller and is now merged with Anheuser-Busch.

This is a very enjoyable tour, where you learn about the brewing of beer and can indulge in some beer-tasting. One Saturday a month is dedicated to a beer and food pairing experience, where different beers are matched with suitable dishes. There is a good restaurant and even a souvenir shop selling SAB branded goods.

32. THE MARKET THEATRE

Newtown was the original home of Joburg's Market, and many of the buildings date back to that time. The Market Theatre was the old Indian Fruit market.

Started in 1976 by Barney Simon and Mannie Manim, this theatre became synonymous with struggle politics and theatre expressing anti-regime sentiments. Some of South Africa's greatest playwrights and their plays were first showcased here, including Athol Fugard, William Kentridge and the Handspring Puppet Company. The last-named fabricated the stunning "War Horse" for the play of the same name. If you cannot get to see a show, consider the guided tour through the theatres, which takes about 90 minutes.

33. MUSEUM AFRICA

Housed in the Old Market together with the Market Theatre in Newtown, Museum Africa is a social and cultural history museum, predominantly about Johannesburg. The collection holds over 850 000 items, only a few of which can be on display at one time.

With artefacts ranging from Ancient Egyptian and Ethiopian art to implements of daily life in the mining town of Joburg, Museum Africa is constantly evolving.

You can also take a tour of the Newtown Precinct, which has other attractions, such as the Sci-Bono Centre and the Bassline, a legendary club where artists such as Abdullah Ibrahim started their careers.

34. FOOD; EAT A BUNNY CHOW

To be truthful, the home of Bunny chow is Durban, but that does not mean you cannot sample one in Joburg. No it is not a salad, nor does it include any rabbit. It is half a loaf of bread hollowed out and filled with a tasty curry - the ultimate street food.

While the best bunny chow is reputed to be had at "Curry and All" in Sandton, you can try your first chow at places like Neighbourgoods.

Why is it called bunny chow? No-one is really sure, although at one time Indians were known as "Banya" and "chow" is slang for food. By the way, Durban has the largest Indian population of any city outside India.

35. MABONENG

Maboneng Precinct is a regeneration project of the inner city. Housed in what was once a run-down and unsafe part of the city, this is now a hot spot to visit and even live.

Maboneng ("Place of Light" in Sesotho) is a hub for creatives, and you can visit their boutiques interspersed with eateries offering everything from Mexican to Ethiopian food.

There are many events on the go, including the Thursday night cycling tour, where cyclists take to the streets of Joburg in the vicinity of Maboneng.

The City Bus Red Route has a stop here.

>TOURIST

36. JAMES HALL TRANSPORT MUSEUM

Also visited by the City Bus Red Route is the James Hall Museum in the South of Joburg. Definitely a place for boys and their toys, over 400 years of transport is represented in this collection assembled by James Hall, starting with vehicles pulled by animals and graduating through to motor vehicles that we are more familiar with.

There are bicycles and motorbikes, including the penny-farthing and some very rare and special sedans, as well as steam driven vehicles and tractors.

The Portuguese restaurant La Parreirinha is less than a kilometre away, if you get peckish for piri-piri prawns.

37. EAT SOME PIRI-PIRI

South African cuisine is very diverse because of the many cultures that populated the country, either voluntarily or involuntarily. Slaves from Indonesia adapted their cuisine to fit the ingredients available, resulting in Cape Malay cooking. Indian, French and Dutch food also contributed to the mix, and there are some unique South African flavours based on the botanical treasure-house of the Cape, such as Rooibos tea. One cuisine that has made a strong impression is Portuguese-African cooking, especially piri-piri sause. Piri-piri is a chili sauce and there are many varieties, ranging from hot to incendiary. If you are not familiar with this sauce, you must try prawns or cooked with it. For those who are not addicted to chili, there are softer options, such as lemon and herb. There are many places to eat Portuguese, we will just mention two.

38. LA PARREIRINHA

You will probably need to take a taxi to find this restaurant (pronounce it "Pa-Ray-ring-ya"!), buried in the heart of South Johannesburg. It is located in an old police station and has been going strong for around fifty years. It is definitely not posh, but the quality of the food is renowned.

Apart from Piri-piri prawns and chicken, you can also feast on caldo verde, the famous vegetable soup, trinchado, a hearty beef stew and finish off with natas, small custard tarts. Wash it all down with a mozambican beer.

There may be posher eateries that serve Portuguese fare, but they do not have the ambience of this spot. The ceiling is festooned with thousands of ties left behind after expansive business lunches. If you cannot get a booking, they have recently opened a fast food outlet nearby, ask where the "Rapido" is situated.

39. NANDO'S

Another Portuguese eatery just up the road from La Parreirinha is the original Nando's, a nondescript takeaway joint, which now has branches all over the world. You may be familiar with Nando's if you come from Britain, but if not we suggest you try a take-away from them (although they also have tables).

Nando's have won their loyal clientele both by consistent service and products and by their irreverent humour. if there is some political happening, Nando's will have something cheeky to say about it. Sometimes some of their ads have been banned from TV broadcasts, but fortunately you can view them on Youtube.

>TOURIST

40. ASCOT PHARMACY

We know how it is; there is always at least one person for whom you have to buy perfume or after-shave when you travel. While this does give you something to do at "duty-free" during the wait to board your plane, consider a trip to Ascot Pharmacy. This very unimposing shop sells a wide range of perfumes, a fact you will find hard to believe when you visit it. Do not go around Valentine's Day, Mother's Day or Christmas, as the shop is packed to capacity then.

You will find that the prices are very competitive and often better than the duty-free shops, because of their low overheads and huge volumes that they sell. They also have an online store if you are staying long enough to take a delivery.

Working in South Africa and the people in Johannesburg get under your skin. It stays with you. It's a place I want to take my children back to. It's a place that filled me with great joy and inspiration but also sadness. I think it's one of the most complex places on the planet.

-Ryan Phillippe

41. 44 STANLEY STREET, MELVILLE

Melville has been a trendy and bohemian suburb for ovr 60 years, and 44 Stanley is typical of the suburb. From the outside it is a rather bleak industrial building, but enter the courtyards within and prepare to be enchanted.

There are interesting shops and boutiques, interspersed with laid-back places to eat and drink. A few of the places you can find here include:-

Lucky Fish - the modern equivalent of a trading store
L'Elephant Terrible Bookshop
The Salvation Café - for breakfast and lunch
Il Giardino - Italian food among the olive trees
Black Coffee - fashion design

But we recommend you just go and visit and do your own exploring.

42. BEAN THERE

One of the shops at 44 Stanley is Bean There, a coffee roastery. Their main business is importing fair trade coffee for upmarket game lodges and hotels, and you can sample some of the roasts they produce. Try Ethiopian beans, the origin of all coffees and naturally low in caffeine.

Apart from the fact that the beans are really freshly ground, sipping coffee while beans are roasting near you enhances the flavour. Cake is served to stave off those hunger pangs.

If you are not much of a coffee drinker, Lady Bonin's Tea is the place for you, they craft teas from organic ingredients. If it is a cold day, why not pop into Chocoloza and have a hot chocolate, while deciding which handcrafted chocolates you want to buy.

43. 27 BOXES

Also in Melville, a few km away from 44 Stanley is 27 Boxes, a collection of containers housing pop-up and permanent shops that always have something new and entertaining. Fashion and interior design are prominently featured, and there is artisanal bread and other goodies for the food lover.

44. SHOPPING: ROSEBANK SUNDAY MARKET

The Rosebank Sunday market is the place to buy all your gifts to take home with you. Based in the roof parking of the Rosebank Mall, you can buy goods ranging from pewter and porcelain to African curios from West Africa.

There are many artists who have their works on display and are quite used to either sending their work to your home or packaging it to take with you on your flight home.

There are also food stalls selling everything from artisanal bread to Malay curries.

If you cannot make the Sunday Market, the curio sellers operate during the week from outside the front of the Mall.

There is also good shopping and eating in Rosebank, which is a conglomeration of malls and arcades. There is a Gautrain station in Rosebank, from where you can embark for Pretoria or O R Tambo Airport.

45. SHOPPING: HYDE PARK

Hyde Park is by no means the largest mall in Joburg, but it is where the well-heeled shop. The biggest branch of the Exclusive Books chain is found here and you can browse there for some books to add to your baggage allowance.

Hyde Park is the oldest free-standing shopping centre in Joburg, but it has gone through a series of revamps to stay contemporary. It is smaller and more compact than nearby Sandton City, and not so frenetic.

You can buy the best of European fashion, beautiful jewellery and new luggage if you are tired of your current baggage. There is also a cinema complex.

The concierge service at the Centre will arrange transport for you if you contact them.

46. WATCH A CRICKET MATCH

It does not matter if you do not understand the first thing about cricket; a day at the Wanderers watching a match is still a lot of fun, even if it is only in watching the antics of the crowd.

The Wanderers Stadium is known as the "Bull Run" and has been home to many international cricket matches.

Remember to take lots of sun-block and a hat. If you know someone who understands cricket, take them with you to explain what a googly, a wide and a no-ball are.

>TOURIST

47. WATCH A RUGBY MATCH

South Africa is a sport-loving nation - in summer, there is cricket and football. In winter there is rugby. Book for a match to be played at Ellis Park (now known as Emirates Airline Park). Whether it is an international or a local fixture does not matter, you will get to sit among local supporters and inhale the vibe.

48. WATCH A SOCCER MATCH

We already mentioned the FNB Stadium. Try and watch a football match if there is one scheduled. Get familiar with the main teams, there are many, but the main two are Orlando Pirates and Kaizer Chiefs (no, the rock band borrowed the name). Pirates are also known as the Bucs or Buccaneers, Chiefs are also known as Amakhozi (Zulu for Chiefs). Once a year there is a match known as the Derby, a sort of Cup Final, which usually involves these teams playing each other, although Pirates have been a bit off form recently.

If you watched the Soccer World Cup in 2010, you will know what a vuvusela is - a plastic horn that emits a sound like a cow with a stomach-ache. No soccer match would be complete in South Africa without blowing a vuvu - you can get one for yourself when you enter the stadium. You will also see fans wearing makarapas - mining hats dressed up in team colours, with bits and pieces - a great souvenir.

49. GO FOR A SWIM

If you visit Joburg in summer and your accommodation does not have a pool, there are plenty of municipal pools scattered around the city (excluding Sandton). You can take a picnic lunch and laze about at the Zoo Lake pool, for instance. If you are a serious swimmer, head for Ellis Park, which is an Olympic-size pool. Most of the pools are not heated and close from April to September, except for a few. Consult the city of Joburg website for a list of pools.

50. ENTER A SPORTING EVENT

There are plenty of sporting events throughout the year, from fun runs to marathons and triathlons. There is also the famous 94.7 cycle race towards the end of the year, the only tricky part about entering it is borrowing or hiring a bike, but maybe you can find one in the Junk Mail and sell it or donate it when you leave. There are a few open water events too, between October and March.

Remember that Joburg's altitude means that there is less oxygen for your body and that you will find it harder going than at sea level.

>TOURIST

TOP REASONS TO BOOK THIS TRIP

- Joburg's amazing weather: Winter runs from April to October, during which time there is virtually no rain. It can be very cold, with overnight temperatures going down to zero, but the days are clear and sunny. Summer has heavy convectional rainstorms, usually in the afternoons, which cools those hot days down.
- The People. While Joburg has about 5 million inhabitants, it often seems like a village. Stand in a queue anywhere, from the supermarket to a sports venue, and total strangers will open a conversation with you. South Africans are well-known for their hospitality.
- So much to see and do. We have left out quite a few other attractions because space does not permit. If you actually run out of sights and events in Joburg (you will need a year), head for Pretoria, which is only 80km away or a short journey on the Gautrain.

GREATER THAN A TOURIST – PRETORIA GAUTENG SOUTH AFRICA

50 Travel Tips from a Local

Natasha van der Schyff

DEDICATION

This book is dedicated to the cultural mixing pot that is South Africa. A country that I have been falling in love with perpetually since my birth.

Also to my parents, Ben and Hannetjie, true South Africans without whom I would not be the person I am today.

And lastly, to Nicholas, who taught me the beauty of my city.

ABOUT THE AUTHOR

Natasha van der Schyff is a young educator and writer who was born, raised, and schooled in Pretoria. She has an honors degree in English Language and Literature from the University of Pretoria. She also has a Postgraduate Degree in Language Education from the University of South Africa.

Natasha started working in 2013 as a freelance editor, writer, and tutor. In 2015, she became a full-time educator, but still endeavored to freelance as often as possible. She still does independent freelancing and contract work, but find teaching a great fulfillment of her passion to make a difference.

Once aspect of Pretoria that Natasha loves most is the vibrancy of the city – around every corner you will find a new kind of person living in harmony with the previous. Pretoria is an ever-changing landscape with many people and passions.

She loves food, reading books, running, travelling, and writing all sorts of different literature. She is currently teaching at a high school in Pretoria. Even though she wants to see all the corners of the world, Pretoria will always be the point at which she orients herself for future endeavors.

>TOURIST

INTRODUCTION

"Getting lost in the world is how you find yourself."

African Proverb

Pretoria might not be on everyone's list when they visit sunny South Africa, but this city is a mere train ride away from OR Tambo International and should not be missed.

Pretoria is a wonderful city that requires little to no effort to enjoy, but please take some precautions. It is advisable to have little cash on you at all times and to keep your valuables hidden as there is crime and pickpocketing in South Africa.

Make sure you use sunscreen and wear a hat and sunglasses as the sun is rampant at most times of the year. I also suggest having a bottle of cold water at hand. In summer, the weather can change from stagnant and boiling to wind and rain in a matter of hours, so make sure you check the weather forecast and are prepared.

There are many different options for accommodation to suit every pocket and checking AirBnB is advised to get the full experience. Pretoria does not have the best in terms of public transport, but Apps such as Uber and Taxify are readily available and affordable.

Even though South Africa has 11 official languages, you can get by quite well with English in most cases – many locals speak it fluently (or at least their own colorful version of it).

Here is a bonus tip before we begin: If you want something to remember South Africa by, don't by curios (souvenirs) from large curio markets. Rather go to a craft store where you can witness the artists make the product.

1. GO DURING SPRING

Most of South Africa is scorching hot during summertime (November to March) and many tourists find the heat unbearable (A morning temperature of 20oC and an afternoon temperature of 40oC). That being said, Pretoria during springtime (September to October) is arguably one of the most beautiful places on Earth. Not only is the weather more tolerable (it is usually between 12oC in the morning and 26oC in the evening), the entire city is enrobed with a Jacaranda tree purple. For about four weeks every year, residents get to witness the beauty of the Jacaranda city. The trees bloom their lilac buds and shed them on the ground, turning the entire city into a purple playground.

The endurable weather also makes many of the activities on this list easier to do as well as more enjoyable. This is also a time that you will experience the people of Pretoria in their post-winter happiness. There is certainly no better time to experience everything on this list. This is also our yearly indicator that the season has changed from Winter to Spring and you will find many South Africans being more jovial as we tend to enjoy summer the most.

However, should you decide to go during summertime, please carry sunscreen and a hat, as well as some water. In winter we generally have moderate temperature during the day, but the houses can get quite cold as none of them have central heating, so be sure to keep warm.

>TOURIST

2. SEE THE UNION BUILDINGS

At more than a century old, this landmark of Pretoria is where the magic happens. Designed by Sir Herbert Baker, you as a tourist cannot enter the buildings, but you can admire its beauty from the spectacular view of the gardens below. Pack a picnic basket and settle in next to Tata Madiba for a few hours. This is also a popular running spot for many people residing in the area. Fun Fact: the Red Bull X-Fighters show was hosted here and made for beautiful pictures.

I saw it for the first time when I was 11 years old. My uncle was in a bad car accident that hospitalized him for several months and his son stayed with us during that time. In an effort to cheer him up, we took him for a day out at the Union Buildings. Now, whenever I drive past there, I cannot help but think of the smile on his face – his first smile in weeks – when we were running down the steps to the lawn in front of the buildings.

The gardens beneath the buildings make for a beautiful spot for a couple or a family to enjoy an afternoon. An interesting fact: the building has two wings joined by a half circle – this was supposedly to show cooperation between the English and Boer ruling factions as this was built just after the Anglo-Boer war.

3. TAKE A WALK THROUGH THE CBD

It certainly is one of the smaller cities (when compared to Cape Town and Jo'burg) but it definitely does not lack its nuances. The

CBD is one of the older parts of Pretoria and still has some of the nuances of an old city. There are many things to do there, but make sure you do this in a group and not late at night. The next few things can be experienced while walking through the city.

As a child, I would drive around here with my father during school holidays and marvel at the old church that time forgot in the middle of the city. However, walking is the only way to truly experience its beauty, as the traffic is horrendous (as with most city centers). You can marvel at the modern mixed in with the classic, as Pretoria was developed over decades of much reform and rebuilding. So, you might find a tiny, picturesque church, dwarfed by a skyscraper.

4. TAKE A STROLL THROUGH CHURCH SQUARE

One of the oldest squares in Pretoria, this sight was once the middle of the hustle and bustle of Pretoria. From here, many of the following activities can be walked to, but there are Taxi or App Rides available as well. Take a step back in the square that time forgot. Even though the design is still quite old century, right now, it is more of a heritage sight with free WiFi than anything else, but it is still beautiful to see.

Before Pretoria was the hustle and bustle city it is today, it was a mere farm town, and farmers used the square to sell their produce come the weekend. It later became the centre of town. Still today, you can view the original post office, parliamentary building, and

>TOURIST

high court of Pretoria from the square. The high court is used today still for the same purpose.

5. VISIT MRS PLES

Mrs Ples is the most complete skull of an Australopithecus africanus ever found. Even though she was found in the Cradle of Mankind, she is now housed at the The National Museum of Natural History and it is a great place to visit the ancestor of all ancestors. Formerly known as the Transvaal Museum, this wonderful mark of our heritage can be found right next to Church Square and is reasonably priced at that. The museum has been a stalwart for the natural education of many learners around Pretoria and provides a day of fun for the whole family.

Saturdays in my house were usually spent next to the cricket field or fishing dam with my father and twin brother. However, one Saturday my father brought us to this museum and it is still one of best childhood memories. Many of their exhibits were interactive when I was a child and I remember spending hours here going from place to place – reading, pressing buttons, and reading some more.

6. SAY HI TO FIRST STATE PRESIDENT PAUL KRUGER

Or at least see where he lived. A visit to the Kruger House is a must when going seeing the history of South Africa. Also situated in the CBD, this house has perfectly preserved the living quarters of the first state president of the republic, Paul Kruger. It is an exciting look back at what Pretoria looked like many years ago and what we have become today.

Paul Kruger is the man that the Kruger Rand is named after. His house was refurbished in 2012. The house contains many gifts given to President Kruger during his life, many of which were supposedly to gain his political favor.

7. GET YOUR HIPSTER VIBES ON AT MARKET AT THE SHEDS

Not only is Pretoria rich in history, it is also rich in food. This is one of the best foodie markets for Pretorians, as well as displaying young artists. The market is hosted at the trendy Sheds venue – an old firehouse turned mall of sorts – and is perfect for your inner hipster. There is safe parking about a block away, and at a reasonable price.

It is a true showcase of the culture of South Africa as it hosts not only foodies, but artists, musicians, fashionistas, and designers. This is a good spot to get a souvenir for your family back home.

My suggestion is to try some of the craft beer on tap here or have a wine tasting with some gourmet South African street food.
My fiancé and I went here to support a friend (Henry Marsh is his name) for his first photography exhibition – three years later he became our wedding photographer and cannot keep up with his workload.

>TOURIST

8. VISIT THE ANIMALS OF THE WORLD AT THE NATIONAL ZOOLOGICAL GARDENS

Don't judge this book by its cover, because this zoo is not in the best location, but it is certainly worth the travel. Find the magic hidden within. This is quite a large zoo, so allow a day for walking around or book a golf cart and take money for the food and drinks available there.

There is a wide array of animals in this zoo, making for an interesting visit.

It is the only zoo with National status and was rated as one of the top zoological gardens in the world. Normally I am not a fan of zoos as I feel they promote animal cruelty, but this zoo is different. The animals here have roaming space and are very well cared for. Many of these animals are also used for research and rare animal breeding, making it a positive contribution to the animal world.

When I was four years old I got a bit up close and personal with nature here and had my first bee sting while waiting in line for the cable cars – needless to say, we did not ride the cable cars that day. A few years later, while on a school trip, I got my first serious burn wound from the cafeteria.

Even though I love animals and enjoyed coming here on school trips (with the aquarium being my favorite), I always avoided the snakes. Now, many years later, I feel very bad for the teacher that always had to sit outside the reptile house with me. Despite the "Oopsies" that happened here, this is still one of my favorite places.

9. TAKE A STROLL THROUGH THE VOORTREKKER MONUMENT

Erected in 1938 at the centenary celebrations of the Great Trek undertaken by the Boer community, this landmark is essential to any person wanting to know the full history of Pretoria and most of South Africa. There is a museum, a restaurant, and a walking tour. If you prefer this mixed with some great rock music, skip to point 10.

My first visit here was another odd Saturday not spent fishing or playing cricket – I remember all the steps we had to take to get to the top of the museum and how absolutely beautiful it was. I am a person who loves historical things, so every step of this museum enthralled me. There are so many elements to this monument that you have to take the time to visit each one of them. There is the Forst Schanskop Museum (which used to be a prison and fort).

10. HAVE A JOL AT PARK ACOUSTICS

Jol – pronounced dj-ohl. Party or jovial gathering of people - usually becoming quite raucous in nature. South Africa has some amazing rock musicians. If this is your cup of tea, go look at artists such as Jereemy Loops, Fokofpolisiekar, and Karen Zoid. Hosted by the aforementioned landmark on the last Sunday of every month, Park Acoustics is every rock music lover's dream.

They have, however, recently been showcasing more indie and rap music to cater to a wider range of South Africans, but their line-up will give you an indication of what to look forward to. Ticket are

>TOURIST

inexpensive, but alcohol can be costly. You may take your own alcohol and food, but not glass is permitted due to safety reasons.

This music festival hosts a different set of South African artists each time and is wonderful to enjoy while sipping a beer. It is a great way to spend a day with friends all while listening to some of South Africa's best musicians. If you enjoy music festivals set in beautiful surroundings, be sure to pay attention to point Number 26.

11. EXPLORE ONE OF MANY NATURE RESERVES

Groenkloof: One great thing about South Africa is its abundance of nature. We love our outdoors and Groenkloof Nature Reserve is at the top of any city bug's list when it comes to walking or cycling. This park is situated close to the CBD and is a wonderful mid-city getaway place for a nature lover. It is also a wonderful spot for a Braai (Br-eye – Go hard on the "r").

Rietvlei: Once again, proof that you can find anything in this city. Rietvlei used to a large farm but has since been changed to a national nature reserve. This mid-city spot is a wonderful outing for the family to enjoy most of the big five, a Braai, or a spot of fishing. Even though it''s not as big as say, the Kruger, you still need a few hours to truly experience its wonder. If you want to walk around here, you will have to do so with a guide as some of the animals here are dangerous when encountered.

Moreleta Kloof: This nature reserve is perfect for long walks or runs and is situated more toward the suburban area of Pretoria, so you will find many families enjoying a day out here. There are many different kinds of bucks (antelope). It also houses a hidden restaurant that is great for a post-hike coffee. There are guided tours available should the need arise.

There are about four more nature reserves in the greater Pretoria area, as well as Dinokeng Wildlife Reserve, but these three are at the top of my quick-visit list.

12. VISIT THE HAP HOUSE

Huis vir Afrikanse Poësie. Directly translated, HAP's name means The House of Afrikaans Poetry. This is arguably the most hidden gem you will find in Pretoria. Featured here are several interesting characters that surround a cultural hothouse. The House boasts the Mimi Coertse Museum of Afrikaans History and is often seen displaying artwork and hosting small cabaret-style shows.

Susan, the owner, can often be found coaxing visitors to try her Turkish Delight Cocktail or selling some of their wonderful food. Sit down in their magical garden and have some freshly baked bread or pasta with a glass of house red.

A family member of mine hosts his annual Pretoria art exhibition here, and it was on one of these occasions that I first came here a few years ago. HAP is quite inexpensive and always has a friendly and vibrant atmosphere with a mix of people. Be warned that you will feel like family.

>TOURIST

13. HAVE A TASTE OF BILTONG

This South African delicacy is available at most butchers and supermarkets throughout the country, but Pretoria has some of the best. It is very much like beef jerky, only much tastier. You can find various cuts and levels of fattiness to enjoy, but it is best served in a social setting with a form of alcohol (I suggest whiskey or wine).

When my brother and I were babies, our parents would soothe our teething gums by giving us biltong to chew on. This, apparently, worked better than any other method. I suggest Mondanette Butchery in Monument Park or Groenkloof Butchery in Groenkloof. Biltong is quite expensive, but it is worth the money.

14. TAKE A DRIVE TO HARTEBEESPOORT DAM

Technically, in a different province, many Pretorians enjoy this dam come the weekend. Affectionately named "Harties", it is a popular holiday spot and is surrounded by an array of things to do.

My suggestion is to find a hidden film backlot called Hartiwood and enjoy an authentic milkshake. Or perhaps take a drive to Jasmyn and the Windmill, a local farmer's market and Dutch-themed restaurant. There is also an animal sanctuary and snake park for the nature lovers.

As a child, my family would go for a yearly visit and I remember when there was just one small shop and a liquor store. Now it has turned into a fully-fledged holiday town with all amenities. But if you look past all the touristy things, there are many farm stall that sell fresh products.

15. GET INTO THE SOUTH AFRICAN SPIRIT AT LOFTUS VERSVELD STADIUM

You cannot visit South Africa and NOT attend a rugby game then you have not grasped the essence of what it means to be a Pretorian. Many South African love rugby and Pretorians are no exception. Loftus Versveld is the home of the Blue Bulls and has a wonderful pub-style restaurant, Trademarx that is a popular spot after the game.

Remember to bring some Biltong to the game. If you would like to stir up some trouble, simply mention the Stormers.

My first time at Loftus was as a child watching my brother play rugby. I remember feeling dwarfed by the massive stadium and having a sense of awe from it. In this stadium, you feel truly proud to stand where legends have made history. Now, I regularly go when my learners are playing.

16. HAVE A GHOSTLY TIME ON THE PRETORIA MIDNIGHT GHOST TOUR

Like many cities around the world, Pretoria has an abundance of skeletons in its proverbial closet. And a few wonderful companies have capitalized on this to provide locals and tourists alike with a spooky midnight ghost tour. This tour takes you around all the sites that have a spooky history and all the creep that comes with them. Be warned that this tour takes place late at night.

You can also have a dining experience in a haunted house that will knock your socks off – but be warned that this tour is not for the faint of heart.

17. EXPLORE THE SCI-ENZA SCIENCE CENTRE AT THE UNIVERSITY OF PRETORIA

From ghostly, to scientifically astounding. The Sci-Enza is a popular destination for students around Pretoria to learn about scientific principles and have some fun in the process. My suggestion is to don the mirror maze or walk up to the Camera Obscura for a bird's eye view of the University.

As a child I remember visiting this on the main campus of the university and deciding then and there that I wanted to study at the University of Pretoria. Ten years later, I started my first year.

18. BE ENTERTAINED AT THE PRETORIA STATE THEATRE

One of the oldest cultural celebratory buildings, the building has theatres of all shapes and sizes and hosts a variety of shows. Be sure to check Computicket for the relevant information. You will find many different types of shows here, from stand-up comedy to ballet.

When I was a young girl, the school that I was studying dance at would host their yearly recitals here. I remember a dress-rehearsal day when the entire student body was practicing for opening night. I wandered off backstage to explore and found a company rehearsing their opera. This is a truly magical place with many hidden gems around the area and is also wonderful for the entire family.

19. GET YOUR SECOND-HAND BOOK ON

Pretoria is a wonderful place for all bibliophiles. You have plenty of nature to go read your books in, and with this many second-hand shops, you cannot but help shop until the books make you drop.

Rutland's: Another hidden gem (even for bibliophiles), Rutland is an old house that has been converted into a bookstore. When they advertise wall-to-wall books in every room, they are certainly not exaggerating. They also do book exchanges on certain titles, so be sure to take your old books. The owners are also quite clued up on everything in their store, so you merely have to ask. In addition, if you are looking for a book, they will try their best to find it.

Doug's Books: Even though these books are mostly second hand, they are certainly not cheap. Doug specializes in finding rare and collectable books for the connoisseur. Many of his books are rare first editions.

PCH Bookshop: This wonderful bookstore is run entirely by volunteers, and benefits the Princess Christian Home for elderly and those with Alzheimer's. They run exclusively on donations and stock most kinds of books at a steal.

>TOURIST

Outer Limits: So this is not technically a bookstore, but they do sell secondhand written works. If you were looking for geek central, you have just found it. They are widely known as the place to go if you have comic book, action figure, or board game needs. They stock a range of new and old comics, as well as wonderful memorabilia for the collector. They also host card and board games, so be sure to visit their website for updated information.

20. SEE WHAT A MILLENIUM-OLD FIG TREE LOOKS LIKE

Wonderboom (pronounced vhonderboom). Directly translated to Tree of Wonder, this 1000-year-old fig tree is protected in the aptly named Wonderboom Nature Reserve. The legend goes that the tree is as large and old as it is, because a local tribe buried their deceased chief at its young roots.

Believe it or not, the tree was much bigger 200 years ago than it is now. There was supposedly a fire that damaged some of it, but some people speculate it was part of the roots that were removed during a plague within the tree. In the Wonderboom Nature Reserve you can find different species of antelope and other small game. This is also a wonderful spot for a Braai or hike.

21. RIDE THE TRAIN IN STYLE

Rovos Rail is a private train company that offers trips to various destinations throughout South Africa. The train-hotel is also the ultimate luxury and can be commissioned for many events. They also do custom packages in case you just want to travel around Pretoria.

Even though they are based in Pretoria they go as far as Namibia and Tanzania. A train ride in the Rovos makes you feel as if you are trapped in an Agatha Christie novel, sans the murder, of course.

A few years ago, dear friends of my mother's decided to get married at the station in utter grandeur. They hosted their reception on the train. Needless to say, the night was a hit. And, in case you were wondering, they are still happily married.

22. SEE THE COWS AT IRENE DAIRY FARM

No person would expect to find a functional dairy farm in the middle of a city, would they? This is the wonder that is Pretoria. Situated right next to Rietvlei, Irene (pronounced I-reen-e) is one of the oldest farms in Pretoria. It has a rich heritage of family farming, even though it is right next to the hustle ans bustle of Centurion.

It produces many dairy products that are almost straight from the cow's udders. They are known for their amazing milkshakes. It sells its milk straight to the consumer at their little shop and has a wonderful restaurant and petting zoo. This is a popular Sunday spot for locals to enjoy a breakfast buffet.

>TOURIST

23. HAVE A CUPPA AT THE AUSTIN ROBERTS BIRD SANCTUARY

Once again, here is more nature, not that it's a bad thing. One thing we Pretorians love is being outside. This Sanctuary is sanctioned from the rest of the nature reserves and parks on this list as it is quite closed off and you cannot do many recreational activities here due to its refuge status. It was named after South Africa's most renowned ornithologist and mammologist. His namesake has provided refuge for birds since the late 1950's and there have been over 170 bird species recorded here.

The sanctuary, accompanied by the Blue Crane restaurant (which makes a mean cup of coffee) is also the temporary home of the Pretoria Liverpool Supporters Club for those who like to balance their fiery sport with some calming birds. If you are lucky, you can see the 8th St. Alban's scouts busy on their premises with some or other fun activity.

24. FIND PETER PAN (OR HAVE MORE COFFEE) AT MAGNOLIA DELL

It is strange to think that something beautiful can come from construction. This picturesque park was the product of a soil dumping sight while the municipality was working of the roads in the area during the late 1940's.

Magnolia Dell park (yes, more nature) is close to Austin Roberts and has a beautiful restaurant in it. The restaurant, named Huckleberry's, is a stalwart for many dog lovers and parents or even just lovebirds. They also have a wonderful breakfast. Try the Wendy Breakfast in my opinion. You will also see the occasional wedding taking place.

The Peter Pan statue was stolen many years ago, but was ceremoniously returned (although the University Residences still steal it every now and then). If you are a set of lovebirds and want to profess your love, try locking it in on the Love Bridge.

Before the Love Bridge was even around, my now fiancé took me on our first date here. This was also, incidentally, my first time at Huckleberry's. I had an early-morning class and he (we were just friends at the time) fetched me from the University and took me here. We still have the same breakfast about five years on.

25. RIDE A HORSE AROUND THE BON ACCORD DAM

Situated in the North of Pretoria, Bon Accord Dam is popular amongst horse lovers because of the Saturday Trail Rides that take place. A two-hour ride is only interrupted by a scrumptious picnic. The man-made dam is almost 100-years and is mainly used by the municipality for irrigation, but does provide for some spectacular views.

It is part of the flatter areas around Pretoria so it is quite an easy ride. There are a few companies that offer this service to shop around. There are also trail rides for people of all ages and experience levels, so no need to feel left out.

>TOURIST

26. PICNIC IN THE NATIONAL BOTANICAL GARDENS

If horses aren't your thing, but picnics are, then you will enjoy the National Botanical Gardens just outside the CBD. These gardens have plants from all over South Africa and the world and you can take a walking tour through them. They are truly magical.

The gardens date back to 1903 and were originally the site of the Botanical Research Institute, but were only opened up to the public in 1984. This is a wonderfully inexpensive outing is wonderful for nature lovers and those who want a break from the city.

The warmer north side has a completely different set of flora to the colder south side, and provides two completely different worlds of plants for visitors. This is also a great spot for a walk or a restaurant visit. There is also ample space for bird watchers and researchers to live vicariously through bird or bush. It also hosts the occasional music concert and market.

27. TAKE A DRIVE TO NKWE

About thirty minutes from the city center, Nkwe is also a wonderful day-trip spot for nature lovers. Many visitors jump off the cliff into the bottomless pit of icy water below and have tons of fun in the process (often accompanied by some Dutch Courage). Many people have tried to determine the depth of the water at Nkwe but no one has been successful thus far. Bring your Braai meat and a cozzie (swim suit) along for the ride.

My mother has fond memories of visiting this place as a young adult and these memories transferred to me. For my 20th birthday, my best friend took it upon herself to organize my birthday party, only asking what kind of birthday I want – I said that it had to be outdoors. This was my first time at Nkwe. We made a pact to jump off the cliff (fear of heights and all). I did so, eventually, after about two beers and inviting a stranger to my funeral.

28. TAKE MAN'S BEST FRIEND WITH.

If you are a furkid lover, then Pretoria is certainly a great place to travel to with them – should this be an option for you. The last decade has seen an expanse in dog-friendly outings due to the great demand for it. Waterkloof dog park, however, has been around for ages.

Waterkloof Dog Park: So hidden and yet so popular – this doggy dream was spawned from an unbuildable section between the houses of the affluent Waterkloof area.It is a daily ritual for many in the area to take their furkids here. It is a slow twenty-minute walk to a pond hidden deep inside Waterkloof. Many dogs love swimming in the ponds that form and dog are mostly kept on leashes until they reach the main pond hidden within. When it rains quite a bit, the unique landscape turns into a series of ponds for all pooches to enjoy.

Walkhaven: Another popular spot for lovers of all things that bark, Walkhaven also offers a wonderful meal will those four-legged children find all the possible dirt to roll in. The Park also hosts Saturday mud-runs for humans and dogs alike as well as pet-

>TOURIST

centered markets. It was created for the sole purpose of dogs getting the best out of an afternoon walk. It spans a total of 22 hectares and has picnic and braai facilities. My suggestion is to take the pooches on a Sunday morning when Walkhaven offers a wonderful buffet. This is the perfect spot to sit and relax while your furry friend stretches his legs.

29. SEE AN AIRSHOW

South Africa is very lucky to boast many airports around the country, and some of them are military. If you are lucky enough, there might be an airshow at one of these airports/air force bases during your visit. Just be warned that all of these bases are in the suburbs and can cause a great ruckus, but is well worth the fun.
- Wonderboom Airport
- Waterkloof Air Force Base
- Swartkops Air Force Base

30. GET A MID-CITY MOUNTAIN BIKE ESCAPE AT WOLWESPRUIT

Another beautiful example of city and nature mixing. Wolwespruit is just off the N1 Highway at Rigel Avenue and offers a wonderful spot for you to flex your mountain biking muscles. All the trails were handcrafted by lovers of the art of cycling and are a single track. This park is also suitable for running. This is also quite a mean cycling route, so pack your big boy or big girl pants. If you want to explore more nature that Pretoria has to offer, see the municipal park and reservations in point 46.

31. ENJOY CROQUET (OR CAKE) AT SAMMY MARKS MUSEUM

This point is dedicated to Dr Noomé, who dedicated much of her time and intellect to the children's literature hidden within the museum. This, in turn, inspired me greatly.

Sammy Marks was a Jewish industrial mining tycoon who assisted many people in need during his life. This mansion boasts 48 rooms (none available for occupation) and still has most of the original furnishing. The museum was opened to the public in 1986. Many buildings throughout Pretoria were named after him and after a walk through this cultural landmark you will understand why. There are guided tours available as well as a prestigious sealed library. But you can also walk through by yourself and just enjoy the history and silence.

32. SEND YOUR TASTE BUDS TO HEAVEN AT CARLTON CAFÉ DELICIOUS

Rachel Botes used to be involved with law, but found her calling for food. And gosh-darnit are we happy about that. This wonderful café opened its doors in 2002 and has been satisfying breakfast and lunch patrons ever. This restaurant is moderately pricey and reservations are recommended, as they are quite popular amongst the locals.

Try a cappuccino and one of their unique breakfasts. They also occasionally have a white chocolate and macadamia nut blondie that your hips might not be too happy about, but your taste buds will thank you for. They have a fresh range of baked goods available daily but are made in limited quantities.

33. SEND YOUR TASTE BUDS AWAY AGAIN AT ALL THE WONDERFUL FOODIE MARKET

Pretoria is any foodie's dream destination, as we love our markets. There are so many to choose from, but for this list I have only chosen three.

Pretoria Banting Market: Banting is very similar to Keto, it is very much LCHF and has taken the world by storm. This market provides fresh, homemade products for people with these specific needs and wants. It is also set against the beautiful botanical gardens, which makes non-banting people want to go anyway.

Hazel Food Market: Continuing on the Foodie journey, have a taste of locally-made food, drinks and fresh produce. This Market happens every Saturday morning and is always show-casing something different. My suggestion is to try some handmade cheese or try the American-style pulled pork burger.

Deep Roots Night Market: Definitely the more hipster option on this list. Here you will find a night out: music, entertainment, fresh food, and innovative desserts. Certainly the best spot for a night out.

34. WHEN YOU'RE DONE THEIR, REACH FOODIE NIRVANA AT AFROBOER

Afroboer is a true fusion of South African breakfast and lunch foods. This self-labelled baker's café is a great and moderately priced spot for people who want to try traditional South African Foods, but with a twist. They provide an array of modern pressed fruit juices while also returning to their African roots. Try the Whiskey Oats and one of their many cakes.

35. FIND PRETORIA'S BEST IN THE HAZELWOOD VILLAGE

Even more good food can be found here. For Pizza, try the Four Cheese at Alfie's, for an epic burger, try The Marilyn at The Burger Bistro. 23 on Hazelwood hosts a hilarious quiz night every Wednesday. This collection of restaurants will surely cause any foodie's existential crisis should they have to choose but one.

This selection of restaurants (most out in the open air) gives one a European feeling of waking around the town at night. My suggestion is to try a different spot for starters, mains and desserts. Whenever my fiancé (who is a chef) has a night off, we will usually start here for dinner.

36. FORGET ABOUT THE WORLD AT DUNCAN YARD

This little collection of restaurants, a bakery, and a few shops, is built in such a way that you will not want to leave. Most of the buildings are enclosed into a cove of winding pathways into stores that you did not know existed. Find some bespoke jewelry or enjoy some meat at Papa's real food.

When I was in high school, I remember my older brother taking me here for dinner at Papa's after an art exhibition. This memory is particularly special, because I hadn't seen him in years – needless to say, the food was exceptional and we spent much of the night walking amongst the shops in the pathway, just having a great time.

37. CLIMB YOUR TROUBLES AWAY

The Climbing Barn is another wonderful spot for the adventure lover. It is special because if the only climbing gym in the Pretoria area. There is an 8-meter roof and instructors are on hand to teach you what you need to know. They recently added an outdoor course for those who find themselves a tad on the adventurous side. The climbing barn is reasonably priced and can accommodate climbers of all ages and levels.

38. HAVE A COCKTAIL AT PROTEA HOTEL FIRE AND ICE

There is so much of Pretoria that is nature and should be accepted as that, but there is also Pretoria's modernizes side. The Fire and Ice hotel is more on the expensive side of things, but is a marvel in architecture. The hotel offers luxury living as well as a restaurant that is open to the public.

Their balcony gives you spectacular views of Pretoria, and this is an upmarket venue, so be sure to pack your high heels and the good credit card.

39. ENJOY JAZZ AND WINE AT PANGEA SALON PRIVÉ

Pretoria, as you know by now, is a mixing pot of the world. This you will find in most of South Africa, but I appreciate this element of Pretoria as it offers a wide range of activities far beyond that which you would think exist in a moderately-sized city.

One of these activities is Pangea. This spot is great for relaxing after a long day at work, and getting your culture meter back up. They do this so skillfully at Pangea, they give you a selection of wines, mix it with fusion foods, and play great music all night. The restaurant is great for impressing a date as it is on the more expensive side of dining.

40. FIND YOUR FLOWER AT LUDWIG'S ROSES

Just on the outskirts of the city, you can find almost any rose here within the rows and rows of flowers. This is a popular spot for florists in their search for the perfect rose and is a wonderful outing for the family.

The restaurant on the premises serves mostly rose-themed dishes (it might not sound that great, but turns out wonderfully) and the property also has an events venue for those who are keen on a party filled with roses (who isn't?).

41. EXPLORE THE MINING TOWN OF CULLINAN

Technically this a town on its own, Cullinan is a beauty and must be counted as part of the beautiful city. It is a town that time forgot; the streets are lined with large oak trees as far as you go and many of the original Edwardian houses are still standing to this day. This place is famous for the Cullinan Diamond and hosts many things to do.

My suggestion is to visit the Cockpit Brewhouse on a Sunday afternoon for live music and the nicest Beef Pie. My best friend and I did this one Sunday afternoon, only to find a very attractive musician singing that day. We found out later he is famous South African Afrikaans singer, Josua na die Reën.

42. DRUM AT KLITSGRAS

Somewhere, on the outskirts of Pretoria, there is a place that fuses African and Hipster in one beautiful picture that is Klitsgras. The venue is family friendly. They often host professional drumming shows in their amphitheater and are great for a night out with the friends.

They have great wood-fired pizzas and a general atmosphere of relaxation while having a drumming good time. I would not suggest wearing light or white clothes as the area is mostly dirt.

43. HAVE A CENTENARY OF BEER AT CAPITAL CRAFT

Capital Craft has over 100 beers on its menu, so it is certainly worth a try. But not all at once please. However, certainly try this wonderful mark of beer. The great thing about capital craft is that they have beer from all over the world – some on tap, some in bottles – and can thus satisfy even the most difficult of beer lovers.

Capital Craft has the best selection of craft beers in the country and offer their draughts in many sizes for all different kinds of people. Their food is also exceptional – my suggestion is the ribs with beer battered onion rings.

44. LEARN ZULU FOR FREE

Grounded at Echo in the Moot offers free Zulu lessons once a week to any willing participant. They also happen to offer some of the best coffee in Pretoria. While you're there, I strongly suggest having a coffee and one of their brownies.

It will certainly aid the learning process as it is rumored that Zulu is easier to speak with a mouth full of chocolatey goodness. Zulu is the most widely spoken language in South Africa and that is the reason Grounded decided to teach it. It is also a wonderful opportunity to connect with more locals in the area.

45. ENJOY AN EARLY MORNING AT THE BOEREMARK

An I do mean early – they open at 5am come rain or shine and only stay open until 9/10 am. This wonderful farmer's market has everything from fresh produce to condensed milk coffee. It's best to go as early as you can if you want good produce or the freshest eggs. It's also dog friendly. This market it separate from the other markets on our list as it was the original market of markets.

This market supports the local producers and craftspeople of the greater Pretoria area and is a great early-morning trip for the entire family. It is also dog friendly. My fiancé is a notorious non-morning person, but HAD to wake up at 4h30 to see this vibrant market.

46. TAKE A HIKE

Again, we have our quintessential mix of Pretoria and Nature.

Oubaas Trail: Situated on the Smuts House Museum Property, this trail (directly translated into Old Boss), it lives up to its name, as it is a retiree length of 1.2 kilometers. This trail is also dog friendly. After your walk, I suggest a lovely cup of tea in the tea garden.

Hennops Hiking Trail: This park technically offers three different routes for you to hike. These range from 2.5 to 10 kilometers. But they all travel along the scenic Hennops River. This trail is not doggy friendly due to the fauna and flora present in the area.

Hedianga: Hedianga is a popular walking farm in the East of Pretoria that has the most amazing views. You can choose between the 5 and 10 kilometer route and take your pooches with for the ride.
Just make sure you follow the signs of the different routes. My quick 5k walk once turned into a 10k trudge to find anything that remotely looks like an exit.

47. GET IN TOUCH WITH NATURE AT ONE OF THE MANY PARKS

Yes, you read that correctly. Even more nature. Although there is quite a lot of hustle and bustle in Pretoria, one cannot deny that there are many places to get away from it.

Burgers Park: Declared a national monument, Burgers Park (named after the fourth President of the South African Republic) was originally a botanical garden founded in the 1870s. This park is a beautiful break away from the city center, where it is located.

Venning Park: This park is not that far from Burgers Park and was once again named after a prominent South African figure at the time of its establishment. It is known for its exquisite rose bushes that seem to offer an oasis in Pretoria's urban Arcadia area. There is also a rosarium with 30 different rose species.

Jan Cilliers Park: Certainly one of the oldest parks in Pretoria, Jan Cilliers Park was dotingly named "Fairy Park" by residents in the surrounding areas. It has a lush gardens with many different kinds of Flora. It also has a wonderful view of the hustle and bustle happening underneath it.

Springbok Park: Declared a National Monument in the 1970's, tThis beautiful spot is situated in the heart of Hatfield (near the Spirit of Tshwane) and is great for walking or photos. It is recognized as a national landmark also has a lovely restaurant for the weary traveler. Try to stay away during the night time, as this is not the safest area after dark.

48. HAVE KIDS? READY? SET. PLAY!

If you are a child, Ready Set Play will make you think your parents have dropped you off in heaven. If you are a parent, this is heavenly. This indoor play area has everything from slides to trampolines with a few noisy toys in between. You can simply take your children here, sit back, and watch their oodles of energy drain out of them and into you.

There is also a seating area for parents to have a Ferrero Rocher Milkshake and perhaps breathe a bit. My nephew had his third birthday party here and I sometimes wish I was young enough to play along. We don't know who loves the place more, me for the Ferrero Rocher Milkshakes, or him with the wonderful play area.

49. TASTE AFRICA AT KAROO CAFÉ

A restaurant with a furniture shop and a secondhand bookstore? Have I died and gone to Pretoria heaven? Not only do they cater for decorators and bibliophiles, but also this café tries its best to teach its clientele about sustainable living. This place is certainly worth the visit simply for the unique manner in which it was built. It also has an amazing menu for breakfast and lunch that must not be missed.

I suggest the breakfast with "skilpadjies" and condensed milk coffee.

The owners have a large dog walking around as well as a few fiery chickens (not for eating), so it might not be best to bring your pups along here.

50. HAVE A STEAK AND PAIR IT WITH A GOOD RED WINE

Vegans: Look away fast. South Africans arguably do few things as well as cooking a steak. It is often what we do during a braai, and is how we love to spend our Saturday afternoons. This is truly a stalwart of the South African delicacies.

South African beef has a bit more fat on it, which adds to the flavor. Have your steak medium rare to get the full flavor out of it. Pair it with a good red blend. My suggestion is the Warwick First Lady. My top steak spots in Pretoria are as follows:
- Moo Moo's (Affordable) Here you can pick your cut and how its done, then your sides and sauces. My suggestion is try the 200g rump, butter basted, with their shoestring fries. Pair this with the Fairview Goats do Roam.
- Papa's Real Food - Their steaks all come your choice of fries, baked potato, mash, or seasonal veg.

- Capeesh- They have a wonderful selection of wines ready for you, try the 300 gram sirloin with a glass of the Wolftrap Red.
- Crawdaddy's- If you like garlic, try the Himalayan Rock Salt or the Transylvania Special. These will have you avoiding Edward for months.
- Prue Leith Chef's Academy- Their menu changes weekly, but often has a form of steak on it. I suggest you phone ahead and book a table as well as ask what their menu looks life. Be aware that this is fine dining so this experience will cost you a bit more than the others on the list, but is well worth the price.

Most of these restaurants will also help you with wine pairings.

TOP REASONS TO BOOK THIS TRIP

Tourists so often overlook Pretoria and this is unfortunate. It is an inexpensive city that has so much to offer to a willing party. These are my top three reasons for visiting the Jacaranda City.

Nature: As stated in many tips, the amount of nature found within this city is astounding.

Food: There are so many foodie spots to choose from within the city that there won't be a hungry person in the room.

History: Pretoria is certainly a spot of great history within South Africa. There are so many things to view when it comes to how we got where we are today.

GREATER THAN A TOURIST- PORT ELIZABETH NELSON MANDELA BAY SOUTH AFRICA

50 Travel Tips from a Local

Michel du Preez

>TOURIST

FORWARD

    I am guiding a world audience that needs to know South African roads, municipal names are still changing (re-named). The globally accepted units are imperial, that temperature is understood in degrees Fahrenheit. Currency for consideration is in US dollars, but there will be times to convert into the South African Rand (ZAR).

    Speed is better expressed in miles per hour rather than kilometers, and the distance to describe surrounding destinations are expressed in miles. In an introduction to provide tips for being a greater tourist, keep in mind that the travelling experience in Africa is like an expedition.
    Change is ongoing, a new democracy is still under 25 years. In our beloved country, people and boarding times are never 'on time'.

    The reception for data roaming, telecommunications coverage are third-world as well as the availability of power (that fits your charging devices, universal adapters highly recommended). With all the infrastructure that is still in development, the people, the abundance of wildlife compensate for the detox of technology.

    The airports are an excellent start, that hospitality is culturally innate, as the transport to the airport is somewhat chaotic at times, and this is why if your luggage is at least checked in on time, then the plane does not depart without you. There are people that are willing to track you down and return lost belongings, to those people who are 'dreamers'.

For international reasons, and tourism mandates, the idea behind Nelson Mandela Bay as a name change is not a replacement. The city for which the International Airport is named, is still called Port Elizabeth, this city has long been associated with historical pioneering expeditions from Portuguese Explorers (see Museum section), the Nelson Mandela Bay naming, refers to the name change of Algoa Bay. The Metropolitan area extension beyond the city (Includes Despatch and Uitenhage) encapsulates the vast space of wilderness as well the inclusion of a struggle hero for which was born in this province, more specifically the rural inland regions of the Bay area, but the name change benefitted my personal experience of being a student about 20 years ago.

Enough of the personal sentiments, another consideration is that this guide is for a fortnight (12-14 days) only if it is spent here and not leaving elsewhere, let's get to being the Greater Tourist in Port Elizabeth!

ABOUT THE AUTHOR

Michel is a business athlete. He is a full time business consultant and part time blogger. He has travel and lifestyle blogs that are centric to his road less traveled approach to life. He was born and raised on a sugar Farm in the Natal Midlands later to pursue his love of the sciences by studying in PE and Cape Town before committing to commerce in the South African Economic Hub Johannesburg.

An avid dancer, tennis coach, golf caddy, he has big dreams to help out with his diverse set of empathetic care and sympathetic expertise. His most important job to date has to be his caregiving for his disabled mother, and supporting his family through farming challenges in the political uncertainty of a beloved country wrenched in agenda.

He writes about the beauty of things always optimistic about the future, and with the sadness comes extremes of happiness and content. That is the study of human moves!

>TOURIST

1. ARRIVING IN NELSON MANDELA BAY (FLYING IS BEST!)

The city does have an international airport, but domestic flights keep it semi-capacity. This makes it a very relaxed arrival, as the speeds and hustle are not comparable to Johannesburg (Which has the most congestion of air traffic in RSA) followed by Cape Town, which is the basis of my above statement. Watch carefully as you descend, the area for which you will be roaming for the next fortnight may all be in aerial sight of the descending Boeing 737.

With this open-plan (The runway and the baggage claim are so close!) welcome, it must be noted that the instant feel of space sets the arrival in the right direction. This is a coastal city, which has its own pace of operating, feeling this immediately upon arrival. Take a deep breath and suck as much coastal air as you can.

The alternative to flying is to consider commuting via the national roads or using bus transit systems (Don't). The roads to get to the Eastern Cape are deep rooted with wilderness and flying gives you that perspective of why the sea routes aren't much of a travel option either. The trip from Durban especially through the Umtata region via East London is not recommended.

The Garden Route was developed because of its Road system (N2 Highway) that spoke to many travellers that would fly to Cape Town, spend two weeks in the greater area, then take a week to enjoy stops along the Garden Route which has breathtaking views, and the Southern Cape is highly-underrated (This is definitely my next book-the Garden Route-for the Greater Tourist!)

2. SAFETY DO'S AND DON'TS

It is South Africa after all (the press does give this nation high incidence rates of crime), and being labelled the "friendly city", puts relief in a country with problems yet this could be the second chance African city that puts that all to rest. There is a big drive to no tolerance policies in different provinces, leaving this coastal city with high emphasis on hospitality and tourism to drive the local economy in this region. Diversity of cultures and population, there are some simple rules to keep your belongings without having to spend too much time with insurance and police reports.

When carrying hand and travel accessories, it is not recommended to leave belongings unattended. Keep the vehicle that you travel in locked when parked, no visible items to be displayed through windows, the best advice is to have important documents and wallets in the boot of the vehicle when going for runs or walks. The country gets heated press coverage on the crime and the theft stories that are very high. But too often I meet scandinavian travellers who probably anticipated the worst, and end up leaving saying that this was paradise, and the news is propaganda from too many visitors struggling to engage at the same time, as our systems tend to serve quality numbers rather than quantity . Probably because the weather is unbelievable.

3. FIRST STAGES OF CHECKING IN

Landing at the Arrivals Airport in Port Elizabeth, there is the option, of picking up your baggage claim, switching on your mobile device that hopefully was on flight mode during the domestic flight,

>TOURIST

and switching on the UBER App to get a sense of the availability of taxi's heading to the Main Beach. The Airport is seriously only 15 minutes of driving from the Airport to SummerStrand, and organizing Uber is the most efficient use of time to get checked-in to your Beach View Hotel Booking.

If you have 45 minutes to go through the process of renting-a-car from your AVIS or HERTZ dealer at the Airport, then that is just as time efficient because you free up the possible time of tomorrow and the possible next 4 days to organize travel arrangements. The Check-in at the Hotel will provide shuttles and services to major sightseeing, but with this series, we get to the local flavour of experiencing your fortnight much like a local would. The savings with the vehicle will be apparent after the check-in at the hotel, and do not forget all the amenities when getting the rental. Insurance and extra's are not advisable to ignore.

I would swipe the American Diners card, Mastercard or Visa to rent a car.

4. DRIVING ON THE LEFT SIDE OF THE ROAD

South Africa has road rules synonymous to Britain and Australian laws. The vehicles will have the passengers seated on the side you are most used to in your home country when driving. The advocation of electric and bio-fuel for the environment are still not apparent even with the countries commitment to carbon-free environment by 2030.

Just keep left when travelling down the narrow roads, as in this country the roads don't have wide shoulder margins, and keep this in mind with pedestrian crossings, and animal crossings even in the built up areas. The most common mistake a foreign traveller might encounter is the traffic light system coupled with driving behaviour that is borderline law enforceable. Keep in mind, that there more traffic altercations at stops and traffic lights as the the traffic police do issue spot fines without any camera detection.

Be mindful of road enthusiasts like cyclists and runners, since the roads are not clearly marked, it is an offence to drive within 2 yards of the bikes. Just remember that there are mostly impatient driver mentality with locals, and the best thing is to just let the bumper riders pass with the indication of hazard lights leading the way.

5. SAY "MOLO" AND OTHER THINGS LOCAL

We have a diversity of languages in South Africa, over eleven native languages, but with the current statistics of this area showing that the white/black/mixed populations being even, this brings Afrikaans as the most spoken language. But the Xhosa tribal greetings will go just as far, by saying hello, everything changes...say "Molo" pronounced (more-law) and this means Hello in Xhosa.

The help is sometimes too much, there are car guards who ask for tips, and I will get to that tip section, but why tip a guard who has no security pass? It's also advisable to watch the approaches to clean vehicles, with the water crisis, it is recommended not to have your

>TOURIST

rental washed in order to get the full refund. Most parking tickets are the only expense necessary for visits at a shopping centre.

It would be more useful when asking for help in the designated areas (Standard Question Mark is encircled for tourist information) for tourism help which was increased dramatically with the World Cup Soccer being hosted here in 2010.

To say hello in Afrikaans, simply say "Goeie dag!" much like Dutch or German speaking accents, just pronounce the "g" with the breakdown of ((g) - coy - er - dah- (g)).

Other really useful phrases are…
"Asseblief, kan u vir my help?"
"Wys vir my, waar is die strand"
"Hoeveel kos die goedkoop?"
"Baie dankie!"

6. CURRENCY TO CARRY

This is where I would highly recommend the non use of cash. Of course the curio shops and informal markets only accept cash, but every mall will have exchange facilities when needing foreign transactions. I would travel with dollars, and swipe the card, as the rate at which the Rand is hedged versus the dollar, it is far more powerful to work in the stronger currency.

As I write this article, I find myself looking at an exchange rate of 15.20 (ZAR) to one US dollar. American Express and Diners Card are readily usable, and the presence of expats at the coastal regions has increased over the last ten years.

If you arrive for a fortnight in South Africa, drawing cash equivalent to the amount of 150 USD could last two weeks if you don't use it for meals at restaurants, purchases or accommodation, or rental costs. In Port Elizabeth you could be eating a three course meal with your loved one, and a bottle of wine, and the bill will end up less than 50 USD!! True story!!

7. WELCOME TO THE WINDY CITY

To give perspective on this destination. The windy city is geographically positioned being the southernmost largest city (Lower than Cape Town) at the tip of Africa.

It is not the point at which the Indian Ocean and the Atlantic Ocean meet. That Cape Agulhas point is more the southern Cape, and then the Eastern Cape province is the most correct description of sticking out for the winds to build momentum off the south and eastern fronts. The windy means that the gusts are penetrating forces of 18 mph probably twice a week.

Hard to compare the severity of these gale force winds as to Cape Town (West Coast). But the Natural growth of trees are very stunted with the surrounding abundance of fynbos.

The temperature of the bay never rises above the 78.8 degrees Fahrenheit mark on average. The wind chill does regulate the ambient temperature, but mostly the chill factors make the temperature colder rather than warmer. The humidity will always be the advent of how the temperature is felt, and the humidity could be as much as 70% with the minimum and maximum temperature never really feeling like the metric.

In summer it gets up to 86 degree Fahrenheit. In winter it will never below 51.8 degrees Fahrenheit. I used to get super burnt because. You could never feel the sun radiating on your skin, it is important to cover with SPF 50, reflected rays from the water accentuate the exposure to UV rays, and wearing a hat does help with the protection factor, but even if the sun is not out, you must apply lotion to moisturize as well as manage sunburn.

8. THE BEACHES ARE FLAT!

Once you have checked in, have your rental parked in the designated garage at your beachview hotel, the scene of the lover's walk coupled with a neat horizon of the Indian Ocean. You will notice. "Where are the wave's?", the beaches here at Port Elizabeth are flat, but that does not mean the activity is flat!

The beaches have a definite signature. The surf and the tides do not have wild coast characteristics of steep tides and surf propensity. The beach is COLD! Cold in South Africa is anything under 20 degree celsius which is 68 degree Fahrenheit.

The cold waves and swimming conditions do pose wetsuits, and surfing is popular at spots like Hobie Beach and Pollocks Beach. But Kite Surfing, longboarding, Surf Kayaks are all super popular. I used to train on the beaches like a lifesaver, and that as a sport is very popular amongst rowing and boat orsman activities.

The wind and the temperature makes the conditions what they are, and for the traveller, the wind created the unique sand dunes, as well as the specific indigenous bush that is around some of the rocky coves and reefs that attract much scuba diving and snorkeling activities. This is all the reason why this is known as the Watersport Capital of South Africa.

9. BOARDWALK

If you have booked one of the Beachview Hotel Rooms with its magnificent views, you are now within walking distance of the boardwalk, and this means you have options to not have to drive your rental if you would like to do the lover's walk and have that Sunday booking for lunch and Blue Water Cafe' options.

The Boardwalk is the closest to a Mall on the Beach, it has very elegant features all in an oasis of a property. Amongst a pond that is walkable to the main beaches. You could park at this centre, quite comfortably visit the casino for sports viewing and restaurants. Then head for the long walk to the piers for some sea views on a Saturday afternoon, the Taverns and spots are all approx 1 mile apart from the Boardwalk, the Main Beach and your parking within the secure Hotel accommodation.

10. REACH OUT ON SOCIAL MEDIA

Facebook, Twitter and Instagram (Use "Nelson Mandela Bay" as search engine keyword) will have variety of activities and locations, where the festivals might be hosted, the Facebook page is open to public, and it is updated real time for you to maybe visit the Festivities at Young Park or even the new Stadium Precinct.

The other aspect of media to follow is the radio, the radio broadcasts to the Internet as well as Algoa FM on your rental stereo, the radio station Five FM are very informative about happenings and gig guides for the midweek or weekend in the bay area.

11. HOW TO GET AROUND

I still recommend that getting around does become cost-effective by renting a car. But that does not stop you from a designated parking area where buses may move masses to a sporting event, or even the options for a train ride that does an inland loop for a different perspective. The open plan Bus (CitySightSeeing) is best for tourists requiring commentary on History as well as a loop around the main beach attractions as well as trips to monumental sites that are situated in PE central.

There are park and ride facilities all over the Summerstrand area, as the trip to PE Central can form part of a trip sanctioned for the Museum or even the Parks and Recreation Centres at St Georges.

If there is a planned event at Nelson Mandela Bay Stadium, I know the best parking would be at the South End Museum (near

Kings Beach). Park and Ride facilities work wonders, and what better way to mingle to locals about their favorite past-times like Rugby. Events are held at the World Cup Venue that hosted a number of matches at the FIFA World Cup 2010.

12. UNIVERSITY ON A GAME RESERVE?

It is shown as NMMU Game Reserve on Google Maps. This would be most useful if time is limited below a fortnight, and the trip to Maitland Game reserve, or even Addo Elephant Park were at the bottom of your to-do list. The University campus as mentioned earlier, which has had a name change does have the most beautiful walks amongst nature, where else can a campus have little antelope springing in between the Campus game reserve.

I do know that the University will also provide tours around the campus, as the sport section is protected by the wind breakers of natural shaped bush which surrounds the greens. The buildings do take a battering from the South-Wester of a blustery wind, and go to the main skyscraper building on campus and take the elevator to the top, the views are not advertised, but being like a local would mean this is the equivalent of the "Champ de Elysees" in Paris with dynamic views of Marine Drive and how it becomes the boulevard through the SummerStrand.

Another great picnic or braai idea would be to road trip away from the University grounds on Marine Drive and park at one of those spots, where you can take in the space, the sea breeze as well as silence. The fires may be a contentious issue, but the boards that

>TOURIST

provide braai areas, will indicate where fires are allowed on the Marine Drive stretch.

The playing fields at the University, the athletics stadium, host of big events locally, but it also excellent for the tourist who wants to put in a fitness session where the option of tartan track and grass track are all there for the middle distance enthusiast. But trail running can be most enjoyed starting at the University, and when you have looped the campus, as well as the surrounding trails, head off to Cape Recife Nature Reserve where there is accessible running trail to the corner of the bay marked with a lighthouse, and excellent photo opportunities.

13. CONSERVE WATER

This is a drought stricken, area, as the population has demanded higher supply, the urban development has not optimally dealt with the fresh water reserves as some first class cities would. The census, is that conserving water even when its not considered a drought zone is still highly recommended.

The harsh winds do have something to do with the reserve or the precipitation patterns, and this is important to consider when utilizing water. (washing dishes, clothes and consumption if water). There was also an awful incident three to four years ago where the winds and the fire danger had spread across the city much like it does in the California Bay Area in the States.

14. BEST TIMES TO VISIT

The Summers are amazing, but the Winter's are not cold, and for the foreigners to have more of available spaces open for specific activities, then off-peak times (when South Africans are on School Holidays or Public Holidays). I recommend Early December, Late April as the best times for a fortnight of more bang for your buck.

The winter's are really not bad, the temperature only asks for beanie, and a full overcoat in two weeks of the year, so this really is a place of diversity with wilderness of an ecosystem, for the sea conditions, the precipitation, as well as the golden beaches with dunes, this can be an amazing Winter getaway. Especially when game farms have higher attendance with winter times, as the spotting of the wildlife is far more simpler than the summer overgrown vegetation conditions.

Winter in South Africa is basically June to August, Summer is November to February.

15. WHERE TO STAY

I would stay at the Radisson Blu if my budget is 50 USD per day, per person, for accommodation. This is a 4 star accommodation on the beachfront, and to experience the mornings with a balcony, that would be best, but you can still get bed and breakfast locations along the beachfront for less than 40 USD per day per person.

But to be like the locals, it's also an experience to check AirBnB availability in the Student Village, if they are on three week or four

>TOURIST

week holiday, then the properties would be advertised on AirBnB hosting sites, and I would then get a local, but very good base to drive to the main beach, but also be on route to take Marine Drive onward to SeaView, which has nature, parking, and excellent views for a road trip, and Marine Drive never lasts for than a 30 minute drive, but going back to the student village, the rooms are spacious and then the grocery shopping will make more sense with the furnished lounge and kitchens that would be available for tourists experiencing.

There is also huge popularity to be accommodated on the game reserve in chalets or self catering units in the bush, if this is your main objective of the trip, I would start the fortnight doing three nights of this and do the seaview accommodation for the remaining time to get a balanced trip of wildlife and sea activities.

16. WHERE TO BUY GROCERIES

In South Africa, the retail stores that are most convenient are located in residential areas, malls as well as the garage stations where you can fill up. Either Spar, Pick n Pay, Woolworths provide excellent value for your money, as the quality of vegetables and healthy living is available with all the stores mentioned, in terms of a budget, for the equivalent of 100 USD, you may purchase quite comfortably a week's worth of meals or snacks, and that is excellent for the in between snacks as well as having catering for yourself when not specifically dining in the same accommodation cuisine.

If I were planning to keep staple food in my self-catering fridge (Milk, Vegetables, cold meats), it would end up being a grocery list of all goods that don't need refrigeration upon purchase, so be wise with your grocery shopping as the space in the self-catering is limited, and if your are catering for family then the Woolworths range serves excellent ready made meals that are portioned for the family.

17. BEST RESTAURANTS FOR LOCAL CUISINES

CTFM- Is the the most under-rated restaurant and is abbreviated as Cape Town Fish Market, uptown cuisine with very high standards of seafood and Steakhouse menu's.

Ocean basket is another excellent chain of restaurants, the seafood is franchise standard, but definitely leaves an memorable experience with its menu options.

Blue Water Café was mentioned earlier, and does the local cuisine in a more home-cooked fashion.

18. LOCAL CUISINES TO TRY

One must consider the local restaurants that are franchised, and have a distinct experience that is not reproduced elsewhere. The Game reserves have Food that I would consider as the gourmet chef's that work at these high profiled restaurants, really do bring an exotic and indigenous flavour to the day if it involved game drives or hiking, but the local cuisine to try involves Potjiekos, Lamb Curry,

>TOURIST

as well as traditional Wors with Pap especially at establishments like Maitland or even Addo Elephant Park.

In South Africa, we are well rounded with global influences like Asian and Indian Food. The stews and the Chicken grills are very popular. So there aren't any clear favorites, but locals keep it simple, they say "local is lekker", that is that you can do a Bunny chow, where mutton curry is served in a half loaf cutout, and this is similar to chicken masala that is served with naan bread.

The local cuisine includes traditional Boer kos (Also known as Afrikaans culture), Curry (adopted from Indian culture) and many British delicatessen like homemade pies, also pastries for high noon tea, these are also displayed deep in our history, as the settlers establish trading posts for barters in cattle, spices, teas as well as vegetables.

The viticulture is strong in the entire Cape province, and trying the vintage from some local wineries is also an experience coupled with the right menu. Craft Breweries have sprung up everywhere, and many are trying their hand at their own label, proudly South African innovation

19. BEST PLACE TO BRUNCH

I would brunch at a golf club, just because of the prestige of the venue, the openness of the historical course at Summerstrand called Humewood and then the oldest Golf Club in South Africa is the PE Golf Club. Having a brunch at one of these golfing venues at maybe attempting a walk around the course or even heading back to the beach with a Nature Reserve Walk in mind are all excellent activities to shake off the three course meals at an abstract venue that I have mentioned.

The coffee craze is also evident in these region, what I mean is that there are qualified barista that can go through the process of brewing their own home blend of coffee. This could be an idea to meet some local barista's and also have a decent meal for brunch with the coffee-tasting experience.

20. BEST PLACES TO GRAB & GO BREAKFAST OR LUNCH

Asking the Radisson Blu Hotel Room service is the best option for Grab and Go, they make more of an effort to pack a snack rather than allowing you to do the buffett routine in the morning, otherwise head to the boardwalk to gather a fulfilling grab and go combo from Dulcé that is a cafe that does health options that consider vegetarian and gluten free diets.

21. BEST PLACES TO GO OUT AT NIGHT

Giovanni's or Tapas are located quite close to the South End Shopping Strip, and these are student hangouts if you are into partying to retro music and the alcohol is generally sold as if the establishment becomes too full to have any seated area remaining.

Thats to party with the locals, the more affluent parties with the middle class will happen at the reception of hotels like the Radisson,

>TOURIST

and there are sometimes excellent ambience at Pubs that serve food much like an Irish flavour of St Patrick's Day with KEGS and Barney's Tavern on the beachfront being the best moment to party with locals, and experience that the pub life will always be popular in a coastal city like this.

Clubbing and the night life probably will be exclusive, and social media can provide information related to open -ended parties, if you are keen on Salsa or Tango Parties, there will be Friday and Saturday sessions that are hosted by various studio's and these are advertised on social media quite clearly.

22. HOW MUCH TO TIP?

15% is far more than average, the repeat tipping of the same waitron is unlikely, but 20% is something not to be repeated, as the higher the tip the higher the complacency for others.

If you are playing golf at Humewood Golf Club (One of the oldest establishments in South Africa) and the only true links course, this is an experience for any travellers that are looking to fit in an extra round, the tips here for caddies are 180 ZAR for eighteen holes and giving the caddy 50 ZAR for travel on taxi's is not a bad idea.

Most of the time tipping is a given when you are seeing the influx of begging or homeless people stopping at the traffic lights, so be careful the behaviour that you enable. I would take whatever you would need to give as loose change to an honesty jar of some sort at most paypoints, as the change does get donated to charities and organizations in a ethically method.

23. SHOULD I TIP TAXI DRIVERS

Yes, it is quite simple to do the tipping on the Uber App itself, but would recommend that if you tip with cash, that you never tip more than 50 ZAR, this is way too much! Also as mentioned earlier carrying cash is not necessary, better to tip 10% or 15% for restaurant waitering.

24. BEST AREAS TO GO SHOPPING

Walmer is a great area for shopping, GreenAcres Shopping centre will provide something of the biggest hub for retail if that's what your trip is about. The stock will not compare to international expectations, but clothing and jewellery shops are suitable if this is where you would like to spend a rainy day.

There are factory stores, where some discounting and bargains are available especially if you are into eyewear, the Oakley factory store is the ultimate destination for those willing to have purchasing power, and gift ideas here will range from footwear to training wear as well as eyewear.

25. THE WATERSPORT CAPITAL

The Algoa Bay Yacht Club (ABYC) is based in Port Elizabeth and has been host to many national and international sailing events. The club has a very active sailing section, marina, convivial pub and excellent restaurant with a great view all combining to make the club

>TOURIST

a number one choice to visit. Competitive sailing takes place every weekend throughout the sailing season and social Wednesday Evening Sailing is open to all. ABYC is conveniently situated within the precincts of the Port Elizabeth Harbour just north of the National Sea Rescue (NSRI) and Port Elizabeth Deep Sea Angling Club.

26. WHERE TO GET A WORKOUT IN

This is the host venue for the IRONMAN event held for the South African series to qualify Worldwide. As I write this article, I am witnessing the historical staging of the 2018 World Championship IRONMAN 70.4 event that has brought the world to this host city over this spring period.

I have some of my favorite routes to share considering the wind and some of the legendary sessions I used to participate in with my alma mater in my track days. The event that saw a major influx of international visitors was welcomed with the amazing visuals of television coverage.

The University provides sporting venues with a nature perspective, where the ground maintenance seems to blend in with the surrounding environment. University Sports like Athletics,Soccer,Hockey, Rugby get most of the attention, but use the Cricket analogy to Baseball and witness a St Georges Cricket Stadium experience. Go watch a Rugby Match at the Nelson Mandela Stadium with the analogy to American Football.

In my rental, I would always keep me running shoes, wetsuit, as well as towels and swimsuits. You never know when the weather tells you what activity you should be doing. Renting bicycles for sightseeing is not something I have seen at Port Elizabeth, the locals would meet up every weekday in Walmer if you were a competitive road cyclist, and the memories of the rides that went into the farmlands, and the greater surrounding areas are truly magical. I once raced in Martina Martinique for an amazing ride, and had the energy to still find a surf swim as a cool down at this untouched beach town, it's a sport-mad town Port Elizabeth, and the Ironman has just enabled the lifestyle even more, and the activities for cross training are highly recommended.

27. BEST BEACH TO TAKE A WALK AND FAVORITE BEACH (DON'T FORGET TO BRAAI AFTER A STROLL ON BEACH)

To Walk across Lover's Walk is highly recommended, it's the Pollock's beach (favorite beach) section to the Hobie beach pier and returning back to the parking area.

I would like to mention something that does not appear on the contents page, and I would suggest at least one braai for the greater than a tourist edition. "Braai" means barbeque in South Africa, and it entails bringing your own brickettes that light up with matches/firelighters. Of course bring your own groceries that involve red and white meats from PicknPay, and there is a grid and braai area on every designated beach with parking. How cool is that? It's a South African phenomenon that can have memories of food and the sea, so remember this especially when familiarizing with locals.

>TOURIST

Say "Tjop en Dop" when asking a retail store assistant when unsure of selecting the right meat for a braai, but the best part is the walk on my favorite beach, the seaview, the lighting of a fire, wearing a hoody because of the wind, and sipping on some local wine with the smells of woodfired meat, this is highly recommended.

28. BEST BEACH TO PARTY WITH LOCALS

Beach party culture is not apparent at this type of beach, the wind arrives in the afternoon ans can bring chaos to tents and some marquees to get people on to the sands, the best to do closest to a beach party is the staged parties that are on the pavements, and the parking lot cordoned off for the masses.

29. TAKE A BUS SIGHTSEEING

The open plan bus, is an excellent way to scout the visual points that were witnessed previously on the aerial flight descent. The red bus that is double decker has high popularity with tourists is a good way to do sightseeing. This could be done earlier in your fortnight, then do the rental on the route that may have been navigated for you.

The Citysightseeing Port Elizabeth is the company that deals with routes of hop on and hop off options, I would look into this, trips are either mid-morning or mid-afternoon and don't sit on the upstairs, as the wind can make it unbearably cold.

30. BEST BEACHES FOR SEA ACTIVITIES

The Bay, tagged as the "Water sport Capital"Surfing Port Elizabeth of Africa, offers unrivalled conditions in addition to an abundance of action packed activities throughout the year. Surf lifesaving, rubber ducking, jet-skiing, canoeing, surfing, paragliding and power-boating events are held on a regular basis. Jeffreys Bay, a neighbouring coastal town, is world renowned as the Surf Mecca of the world and is home to the world's best right hand surf break. Jeffreys Bay also hosts the annual Billabong Pro Jeffreys Bay, which draws the world's top surfers each year.

Port Elizabeth is also home to scuba diving (with some spectacular reefs to choose from), game fishing charters as well as other types of fishing, windsurfing, kiteboarding, and snorkeling. There are a number of dive centers to contact to organise a trip out, and various fishing operators to choose from. All hire out equipment.

Sailing is a popular past-time and you will find all kinds of craft out in the bay on a good day. You will often see yachts, catamarans and canoes gliding through the warm waters, creating a wonderful visual if you are gazing out over the bay. There are many cruises offered from the harbour, from sunset cruises to view dolphins to whale watching tours.

>TOURIST

31. NOT INTO BEACHES? TAKE A HIKE

The hiking trails will not include mountains, so be prepared for the walks in amongst indigenous paths and coves that can have magical views especially if the wind and the sunset are on the menu.

Seaview has all the magical hikes, and these would be lining the castland that does not have sand on the beaches, but the natural rocky undulations surrounding some of the quiet beaches located along seaview and schoenmakerskop.

There are no mountains, like Cape Town with Table Mountain and Signal Hill, Port Elizabeth is flat, you will have to be creative as to designing routes and parking spots, SeaView and Maitland were covered extensively on television with the IronMan event, and also excellent to have that out of city feeling when taking the hike.

32. MUSEUMS AND AN AQUARIUM

The PE Museum is must see, but there are various monumental pieces that are established by government as national heritage sites, there are number of these in the settler's way, but take the time to understand the history of this Port, as it was the British colonies migrating from this point of naval strength to venture against the harsh landscapes of the inner regions of the Eastern Cape.

The Aquarium does not have high ratings, but a visit to this venue will give info on how to whale watch and head towards the Great White Shark Adventures. The Sea does have initiatives for volunteering as well as doing programs that involve boat trips and upcoming tide reports and weather broadcasts.

33. GAME FARMS

Addo Elephant Park as well as Maitland Game reserve are highly recommended. These trips inland require at least minimum three nights accommodation that will give you the full itinerary within the Game reserve. The locals don't do the big five game watching, but it is a must if you have never experienced gamelife and what the big fuss is about. Winter is the best for viewing as the vegetation hides the nocturnal habits of most of the wildlife. Elephants are being put on high alert worldwide, and this is an internationally acclaimed Game Park, and this will provide accommodation, activities within the park, as well as dining and experiencing the local cuisine.

The recommendation is to spend time both inland and also at the coastlands, it is a fortnight of travelling here, I would make sure it's a balance between the land and sea activities.

34. HARBOUR AND STADIUM PRECINCT

Try the harbour (There are organized boat cruises, that do booze cruise), with an intention to dine or having another perspective of the bay. The total stretch of the city on the beachfront does stretch 10-11 miles of developed estate, and many more developments are set for an increase. The hotels, lifestyle estates are all in high demand with the wealthier professionals choosing quality of life for the balance of nature with a growing port of industry.

>TOURIST

Not so far from the restaurants on the harbour and yacht club, the World Cup Stadium is in view of this Harbour, great idea to start your midday brunch, and head to the Rugby in the Afternoon from the Harbour, not a bad idea.

35. ST GEORGE'S CRICKET FESTIVITIES

One local activity that may be overlooked, if you are travelling between spring and autumn is the ambience and culture of domestic cricket at St Georges Park. Everyone who does not know cricket will find similarities with Baseball. The sport itself is not the action attraction, the crowd on the West End know how to orchestrate a band festival whilst the sport is on the go.

Visit this venue for a morning or even an afternoon, the culture of the band is a tradition that has last decades, and the locals mix with the diversity at the stadium and it becomes a flavour of Music at the heart of this beating sport that creates neutrality blending different followers of the game to gain more memories of this iconic scene.

The Test Match over New Year's is normally Cape-Town, but sometimes the lucky PE fans can expect the national side to play over the New year, and when that happens you can fill that 20,000 capacity setting at the historical ground that has many annals of sport recorded there since the early 20th century.

36. PACK LIGHT, BUT PACK DENIMS

This is a personal tip. Since the weather is mostly windy, the sun's influence is always negated by a wind chill factor. The denim jeans are a daily staple for comfort wear, you cannot go wrong with this, as it covers the full length of the leg, and obviously the next trick is to avoid dampness, which is highly difficult in the rainy season. Port Elizabeth does not really have a rainy season, but it does have winter rainfall if you are attempting a quiet quick stay without the national holidays.

37. IN YOUR RENTAL CAR, PACK EXTRA PLASTIC BAGS

You never know when you would like to use a possible plastic bag trick when taking off or putting on a wetsuit, the struggle is that you need the slip technique to achieve the fitting of the suit.

The plastic bags are also handy when shopping for groceries, when you need packets that you do not wish to purchase. The other function for plastic bags is to collect litter, the beaches are in great shape, but if we all did our job then the rubbish would have less chance of being blown to areas that can lead to sea litter or even suffocate sea animals in their habitat.

>TOURIST

38. WHEN DRIVING IN A BLUSTERY WIND, DO NOT ACCELERATE YOUR SPEED.

The rental car in this fortnight could head towards spots like Jeffreys Bay, Storms River or other locations which have high rise structures for the highway. No-one really talks about what a crosswind can do to the vehicle if it increases its speeds.

The guidelines on the road signs is to decrease your speed to 60 mph and this is to reduce the possible drag that would lift the possible vehicle into more danger.

39. GO SPEND A FEW NIGHTS ON A FARM (SCHOENMAKERSKOP)

The AirBnB is available in this region, its 20 minutes out of town, and this farmland is mostly dairy, cattle and some lamb farms, but to stay in one of the guesthouses would bring another type of hospitality to the trip. The locals call it the "platteland", the simple life, and the farmers are a community of high empathy, and definitely worth a two night in amongst the fortnight.

40. WHAT IS THE BIG FUSS ABOUT GREAT WHITE SHARKS?

The whale watching is popular, the South Right does breach around the October months, but the latest craze is to shark cage diving, and this stemmed from the pioneering projects back in 2004 in the Southern Cape, where there has been international curiosity around this close encounter with an ancient predator.

To have this variety of wildlife that extends from the Game reserve, and travel out with a boat to observe the ocean in its deep beauty. The cage diving is not necessarily in P.E., but sightings and smaller groups of companies are making efforts to bring travellers closer to higher to nature, and for adrenaline junkies, this includes the scuba diving for treasure off the schoenmakerskop reserve.

There is also big interest from international travellers seeking the storms river bungee jumping, and this cage diving is en route past this bridge for a good day out for sea adventures.

41. WHAT IS THE BIG FIVE?

The majority of visitors think that the big five (Lion, Rhino, Leopard, Buffalo, and Elephant) is only available in the Kruger National Park. This is false, the game lodges across the country are taking a rehab stance on having the game in their domain, but dehorning the rhino for poacher protection and most establishments even in the Cape can have the big five, but the troops of wildlife will be roaming in the game lodges like in the Kruger Park. The animals here are still roaming but it's more of a zoo or rehabilitation from being orphaned that is the expectation needed for game drives.

>TOURIST

42. LIVE LIKE A RESIDENT IN A STUDENT VILLAGE

If you are travelling between June and July and December. The Student houses that are accommodation for six rooms with en-suite bathrooms are excellent if you are booking for groups that are travelling together. Living like a student means that everything is in walkable distance, but this is really for the group bookings example, and I would consider the hotel by the beach as the option for less than three travellers.

43. TRY JEFFREYS BAY

This could be a day trip from your PE accommodation or it's an arrival in the afternoon, braai in the evening, one night's stay at a bed and breakfast in "J-Bay", early morning surf, followed by brunch, and you could be keeping it real and heading back to the Nelson Mandela Bay to continue the fortnight.

44. WHAT IS THE REDHOUSE MILE

This is annual swimming race, mass participation race its held every February, well attended, and on the same scale as the annual Boatrace (Inter-varsity rowing), this is in Port Alfred, and is late August heading into Spring time. This river gets many fisherman and sport activities like water skiing and wake boarding.

45. GRAHAMSTOWN ARTS FESTIVAL?

This takes place around July, and this festival has a week of indi- and alternative talent that stems locally and internationally.

The week has stage and theatre, dance, cultural arts exhibition, very easy to be sucked in for the week. I would arrive in the afternoon, check in at a bed and breakfast, watch a few evening theatre productions, rest up, do an early morning perusal of the markets, and make a move back to the bay with the rental, and drive slowly, as the road trip has great biltong and curio stops. The distance between Grahamstown and PE is approx. 110 miles, so expect to fill up on gasoline en route, and plan for two plus hours of driving.

46. SAND IN MY POCKETS?

With the persistent wind, sand ends up everywhere. I read another Greater than a tourist piece where the solution was baby powder, and it really is the best solution.

47. CARRY VASELINE AND MOISTURIZER

Surfing underarms and swimming irritations. Does not matter whether you are athlete or obese, the skin gets dry and the rash from repetitive over arm over shoulder motions, the vaseline solved all my problems.

>TOURIST

Moisturizing always necessary after a fresh water shower after beach, as the skin irritability scales get tipped off scale when there is dryness.

48. MR MIN AND MY DIY

Anti-Rust and protection from the sea level proximity. I would spray any metals if rain or moisture came into equipment. Keeping this spray is a DIY fix that you won't be able to leave with the cannister whilst flying, as local airlines ban spraycans with its flammable contents.

But theses (DIY) "Do it yourself" methods, are available at convenience stores as well as garage stores. I used to get rusted golf clubs, rusted spokes on a wheel, so this tip really extends itself beyond rust prevention, and is a excellent way to keep your metals from corroding in the sea air.

49. SAY GOODBYE, SAY "TOTSIENS!"

As its always very difficult to say goodbye to an extended fortnight. Remember to thank the locals with the current phrase of Totsiens, since we will meet again.

50. SUNSETS ARE UNIQUE IN THIS CORNER!

Of all destinations, consider the time of the year, and this tip of Africa poses a sunset that is highly competitive with Cape Town, with the horizon being the Indian Ocean, I believe the sunsets to be unique in that no land blocks the setting on the western front, being the only city that can boast Indian Ocean and be the southernmost tip of Africa. In summer time expect those 8pm sunsets to leave an African stamp on a beautiful stay in the windy city.

>TOURIST

Greater Than a Tourist – Sunshine Coast Route Eastern Cape Province South Africa

50 Travel Tips from a Local

Kim Irvine

DEDICATION

This book is dedicated to my son, Quay, who has the biggest little heart and always makes me proud. My brother Shane and his wife to be Gillian, My sisters Dale and Lee you are the best siblings one could hope for and I feel truly blessed to have you all in my life,

My nieces Tia and Mya you girls stay as sweet, loving and caring as you both are. My nephew Ty you are really becoming quite the young man. My soon to be nephews Connor and Tristan welcome to our big family! My parents June and Francis for always being there when I needed you! My brother-in-law Hayden who never gives up on a dream and works tirelessly towards his goals! My brother-in-law Nick always quick with to break up a tense situation with a witty come back. And finally to my best friend Carla thank you for always being there no matter what. Then last but certainly not least to my God daughter Jade you are my inspiration.

ABOUT THE AUTHOR

Kim Irvine is a professional working mother who lives in the Eastern Cape of South Africa with her close family and friends. Having been born and grown up in the Eastern Cape she has explored the many unique and well documented places of the Eastern Cape Province. Her love of life, people, travel and thirst for knowledge has her and her son going on many a holiday adventure far and wide. Having travelled extensively in her twenties and thirties the experience has given Kim an insight into what it is like for a tourist in a foreign country and how confusing it can get trying

>TOURIST

to figure out the best routes to take, places to stay and things to do. Having hosted many of her European and American friends in South Africa she used both her travelling experiences and that of her foreign friends to write this book. Kim hopes to make things a little less daunting for others by offering them reference points and tips for their trip along the Sunshine Coast Route, Eastern Cape in South Africa!

>TOURIST

The Eastern Cape with its mountains, forest and rugged coastline make it the adventure province of South Africa.

With some world famous beaches, malaria frees game parks and various mountain ranges it has a lot to offer both locals and tourists alike.

The Sunshine Coast Route in the Eastern Cape Province of South Africa stretches from the Tsitsikamma Forests to East London or Buffalo City.

The route follows the N2 Motorway from Tsitsikamma Forest to where it joins the R72 some kilometers out of Port Elizabeth following a five hundred kilometer stretch of shore line to East London.

This sun drenched area of the Eastern Cape has many little sea side resorts and villages along the way that offer a host of things to do and experience in a way that is truly unique to the Eastern Cape.

With a high emphasis on family and old school values the people are mostly warm, friendly and always ready to lend a hand.

Whether you are looking to reconnect as a family, have an adventure with your loved one(s) or a single traveler there is a place for you!

You may arrive in the Easter Cape a stranger but you will always leave as part of a close knit family!

1. STAY AT STORMS RIVER RESTCAMP

Wooden chalets are perched all over the camp and mostly with a sea view, the ones I have stayed are almost right on the beach.

At night you fall asleep to the sounds of the sea, night birds and other nocturnal animals and although I never ventured on any the reserve offers various guided night tours where one gets a whole new perspective of the reserve.

There are a lot of fun things to do there and one of my favorites was the black water tubing a five hour river adventure that slides down rapids, swirls around bends and has you screaming and laughing at the same time. It is quite a strenuous ride so should one decide to try it ensures your guide is aware of any limitations you may have.

Although I have never done it myself for those that love camping I believe that both the experience and facilities at the Restcamp are exceptional and makes a great place for a family looking to reconnect.

2. CROSSING THE GREAT DIVIDE – STORMS RIVER

The Storms River bridge was commissioned in the mid nineteen fifties to join Port Elizabeth to Cape Town and to me this is the point that clearly defines where the one province ends and the other begins.

Standing on either side and looking over the dark moody Storms River allows for a unique view of the stark contrasts in not only the climate but the vegetation of the two provinces.

I never miss a stop at the friendly service station, where you can fill up your vehicle, or just have a pit stop to get a beverage, sit at one of the picnic tables and enjoy the view or if you are feeling up to it take a hike on and around the truly remarkable structure.

There is a nice curio shop and some really nice works of art on display for purchase and of course information on the bridge itself!

3. BEACH DUNE SAFARI AT OYSTER BAY

I was not very enthusiastic about taking a dune beach safari but I was very pleasantly surprised not only it is fun being bounced about whilst zooming up and down the beautiful beaches and dunes of Oyster bay or stop to have a picnic lunch atop one affording the most breath taking views but you get a whole new appreciation for the delicate balance of our eco system.

The reserve has many endangered plant species growing within and if you lucky you get to see the African Oyster Catcher which is one of the main concerns of the reserve.

If bird watching is something that interests anyone the reserve is also home to approximately one hundred and seventy different types of bird species.

4. CAPE ST FRANCIS FUN

Out of the coastal villages dotted between Storms River and Port Elizabeth Cape St Francis is one of my favorites.

Not only does it have sandy beaches that stretch for miles that offer fun dune boarding, lazy sun soaks or beach horse rides but it has the Seal Point Lighthouse that was built in 1870's where you get to relive the structures history and stories of the many shipwrecks to occur near the point.

Sharing the lighthouse grounds is the Penguin Rescue and Rehabilitation Center. Where you get to experience what the center is doing for these birds especially the endangered African Penguin and one of the biggest delights for the kids is as you drive in there is a giant penguin statue!

5. NIGHT-TIME FROG SAFARI - CAPE ST FRANCIS

Sporting gumboots, armed with a flash light and net in the inky darkness of the wetlands you get to wade through weeds on a hunt for endangered amphibians.

We pottered around for quite a while before spotting our first one and it is thrilling but at the same time sad to think they were once in abundance and now dwindling due to the disappearing wetlands. The frogs are listed once caught and then gently released again.

Not only is it educational but great fun combined with a good meal and hot beverage when done.

And a great feeling that you may have made a little bit of difference in the fight to save our delicate eco system!

6. SURFS UP IN JEFFERYS BAY

This little town will always be known for being one of the world's best surfing spots and gives hosts to international surfing events where competitors from all over the world come to take part.

>TOURIST

The town has so much more to offer than surfing and being blessed with a climate that has about a five degree Celsius difference between its winter and summer weather makes it the perfect place for a beach vacation all year round.

I love the little shops that line the town center as you can get all sorts of trinkets and shell keepsakes but what I like best is the food; a feast of homemade baked and traditional farm style meals.

If I am looking for bargain brand name surfing clothing Jefferys Bay has factory outlets for most of the big names like Billabong, Rip Curl, Lizard, Quicksilver and Roxy.

7. DOLPHIN BEACH FUN – JEFFERYS BAY

It is always nice to wonder down Dolphin Beach and collect shells. The kid's love it and competition to get the biggest or weirdest one is bound to start by the time you are done there is a sand bucket full.

There is also fun water slides for the kids and surf schools hosted by pro surfers, who will also teach you how to kite-surf or wind-surf.

If, like me, those particular water sports are not for you Dune boarding comes highly recommended but be prepared to get really covered in sea sand!

The little shell and surf museum has many delights to see and interesting little tid-bits that amuse the kids.

I have spotted both dolphins and during July months a Southern Right Whale or two.

8. PARTY ON THE PARTY BOAT IN JEFFERYS BAY

The Jolly Dolphin Party Boat is a very popular spot in Jefferys Bay especially for the younger crowd looking for some night life or to listen to live music.

There are always theme nights, live bands including some internationally acclaimed artists or dance music to party the night away too.

I have eaten here a few times and have really enjoyed my meal with the added bonus of fast friendly service.

As always there are good views no matter what the weather may be doing.

9. ANNUAL WINTER FESTIVAL IN JEFFERY BAY

Every July Jefferys Bay hosts the JBay Open Surfing event where contestants and visitors come from all over the world to compete and partake in.

As the festival offers all sorts of events such a mountain bike challenges, fun runs and more there is something for everyone to do.

Various market stalls setup for those who want to browse and the coffee shops offer their finest food and beverages.

The evenings are filled with live entertainment and fun.

Most that have experienced this festival go back each year time and time again as it is a truly unforgettable experience.

>TOURIST

10. SOAK UP THE PEACE AND TRANQUILITY

Marina Martinique with is it's man made sea water canals and many fun filled activities on offer for the entire family offers five star accommodation at very affordable prices.

Being only five kilometers from Jeffery's Bay makes it good value for money, the high security gives peace of mind and the relaxed atmosphere makes it the perfect holiday destination for exploring the Sunshine Coast between Tsitsikamma and Port Elizabeth.

Aston Bay, the village adjacent to the Marina, offers many excellent restaurants, family Bed and Breakfasts and great fishing spots.

Did you know The Sunshine Coast is named so because it gets the most sunshine in South Africa with around 320/365 days a year?

11. BAYWORLD OCEANARIUM

Fur seals show off their talents as they perform for the audience.

Various species of fish drift around large low lighted sea water tanks giving one a glimpse into the Algoa Bay marine life.

A green house of reptiles and amphibians allows one to experience the ambiance of these creatures habitat.

Delightful Black Footed penguins potter around and interact.

Guided tours are available at certain times during the day which allow for interaction with various animals in a controlled environment.

I do advise to check the Oceanarium opening times and availability as it has been under-going renovations in an attempt to bring back the ever popular dolphins.

12. RELAX AND TAKE A PRIVATE TOUR OF THE CITY

The best way to see the attractions and get to know the best beaches and local places in Port Elizabeth is to take a private half-day tour.

This four hour drive around the city is well hosted and informative in the comfort of a private spacious mini-van.

The stops include various places to visit like the local Museum, Donkin Hill Reserve, Fort Frederick are but a few attractions along the way.

With the reference points in hands once you have done the tour it makes it a lot easier to map out where you want to go in Port Elizabeth as even I find the road systems in the town a bit confusing.

13. CUDDLE A REPTILE, MEET A MEERKAT OR GET CLOSE TO A CROCODILE

The Ado Raptor and Reptile Centre is a small sanctuary that specializes in animal recovery and rehabilitation, just a bit of a detour off the route, they care for sick and injured birds of prey (or raptors) and reptiles.

. There are daily shows and tours where you can get to have a bird of prey perched on your hand as they have up to twelve different species of birds such as Kestrels, Buzzards, Crows, Hawks, Owls and Eagles.

Although not for me one can handle some of the snakes such as the Pythons, anacondas while learning about the other venomous snakes on display.

The center has quite a selection of animals to see from the Nile crocodile to a cute cuddly bunny and the inquisitive Meerkat.

14. BIG TO SMALL ADO ELEPHANT PARK HAS IT ALL

A bit of a detour off the route but well worth the time the Ado Elephant Park is well worth the trip.

The park is not only home to the Big 5 but has a marine section where you can see the Great White shark and seasonally the Southern Right whale.

There are all species of buck, zebra and the very unique endangered flightless dung beetle.

A picnic or stay over in the park allows for a true African bush experience as the animals sometimes wonder really close and the elephants have been known to invite themselves to a picnic or two.

At night you are treated to the African bush symphony of the night creatures, with a million stars overhead adding soft silver lighting as you watch the creatures of the night come out to play.

The guided tours are fun as you bounce along the park in the vehicles taking in the well informed guides words.

15. NANAGA FARMSTALL WARES TO WET THE APPETITE

Where the N2 Highway Meets the R72 along the Sunshine Coast route is a farmstall well worth the stop!

The food is all old home style cooking with the freshest of ingredients including their freshly brewed coffee.

They have quite a selection of mouthwatering jams, relishes, chutneys and preserves.

Homemade fudge, cakes and tarts but one of their pies is an absolute must! They are very well know in the Eastern Cape and have the most delectable pies!

The gift shop carries jewelry, candles, cards and pottery most of which are hand made by the locals.

Try a koeksister, for anyone with a sweet tooth you will not be disappointed, they drip with syrupy goodness!

16. CHICORY AND DUNE FIELDS AMIDST SUBTROPICAL COASTAL FORESTS

Alexandria is a small historical farming town that produces chicory.

Not far away from the town is the Alexandria subtropical coastal forest preserve which stretches to Alexandria Dunefield which lies within the Woody Cape Nature Reserve and one of the largest active coastal dune systems in the world.

The Woody Cape Nature lodge offers both camping and chalets for those who just want a nice weekend away to unwind and reconnect with nature.

Do stop at the various farmstalls along the way if you can as some of them have great biltong if you want to try one of South Africa's meaty snacks!

17. KITE BOARDING AND BEACH FISHING

Cannon Rocks is a well known Kite Boarding spot and the place to be during the annual Cannon Rocks Kite boarding Classic Competition.

The competition shows off the incredible skills of the competitors and even for people who do not generally follow the sport it is really thrilling to watch.

The festival has a great vibe with braai's, beer tents and fun in the sun atmosphere.

Sit around a camp fire in the evening with a guitar and good company beneath the clear night sky.

The local restaurants usually have live music and are a great place to mix and mingle with people from all over South Africa.

18. INTO THE BIG BLUE

Boknes is a very small sea side village that sits on the Boknes River and is a more in season place to be.

It is a great place to find river and sea cruises, scuba diving and snorkeling all offered by the Big Blue Charter company.

Although not one for fishing I have been told that the Big Blue also offers deep sea fishing from the Boknes area.

If you are in the area during the summer season this little village bursts with life as holiday makers come from all over to enjoy the sun and surf.

19. A BIG NEW YEAR IN A SMALL TOWN

Kenton-on-Sea is pretty much like all the other small villages dotted along the Sunshine Coast Route.

With loads of water sport, horse riding, hiking and a restaurant that offers spectacular views and food.

During the December season Kenton is the place to be – well if you can find accommodation that is, or for those who enjoy camping there is always space for another tent.

The locals are relaxed and come together in a sea of endless social functions, braai's and activities that encourage the participation of the whole family.

It is also one of the best places to be to enjoy a truly festive summer New Year!

20. BOAT RACE FESTIVAL

Whether one likes boat racing or not the Port Alfred Boat Race Festival is the place to be.

Spread over a weekend students come from all over the country to compete and camp.

Live bands and various artists from all over the country line up to ensure a weekend of non-stop entertainment and fun.

The race itself is held on the Kowie River where schools compete to win the title in an Oxford / Cambridge style race.

21. A LITTLE BREWERY ON THE RIVER

The Little Brewery On The River in Port Alfred on the banks of the Kowie river is a historical stone building which in itself has a story to tell.

The Gastro pub adjacent the brewery has walls full of Port Alfred history, with brick walls makes it a truly unique place.

They offer good food and homemade beer in a friendly atmosphere with a great view.

"One of the great things about travel is that you find out how many good kind people there are." – Edith Wharton

22. CRUISE THE KOWIE RIVER IN PORT ALFRED

There are a few river barges to choose from and most offer good food, bar and guided tours.

If you really want to experience the river then take the Kowie Canoe Trail a three day trail that takes you past various attractions such as ship wrecks and the reef.

There are also catered and self-catered house boats for hire and its fun to camp out on the river for a night or two.

23. WONDER DOWN HISTORIC WHARF STREET IN PORT ALFRED

This exclusive shopping center stands on one of the oldest commercial streets in Port Alfred and was once nothing more than a dusty old path.

The Wharf Street Brew Pub and Bistro is located in what was once the old harbor office and offers Greek, grills and seafood, the prawn curry is really good.

I enjoy the fresh fish market which has a very good selection of fresh catches and various sea foods.

There are other restaurants and shops with on-going development of the complex to add more outlets.

24. FISH RIVER SUN INDULGENCE

Situated at the Fish River Mouth this luxury hotel offers a host of family entertainment.

The Gary Player 18-hole parkland golf course is rated one of the best in South Africa.

After a grueling game of golf it is great to relax and be pampered at the Body and Beauty clinic spa.

Then round off the evening with a braai and sun-dowers at the Cabana bar right on the beach.

25. MPEKWENI BEACH HOLIDAY RESORT

I have stayed in one of the villas and they are really first class and come fully equipped.

The holiday resort is jam packed with activities for everyone to partake in I especially enjoy the paintball and Dune boarding on offer.

The resort also offers fishing, sunrise or sunset barge cruises up the Mpekweni lagoon, mountain biking, horse-back riding, and canoeing and during the peaks season there are always various planned events that not only bring the family together but are an excellent way of mingling with your resort neighbors.

26. LOCAL CRAFTS, ART AND TASTY TREATS

Between the Fish River and East London along the route is the Bira Craft Market.

I love wondering through the various rooms of the market as they have all sorts of hand-made crafts, art, jewelry and even some furniture.

All sorts of different preserves and homemade tasty goodies are on sale.

There is a wonderful tea room and visitors are invited to write on the wall which is filled with messages and names of people who have visited the market.

It is a great place to buy traditional curios and keepsakes of the trip.

27. EAST LONDON AQUARIUM

My child has been to the East London Aquarium so many times but each time he goes there it is like he has never been before.

It might be small but it has a big impact on a person!

All the staff are friendly and always willing to tell you about their charges and let you help them feed the penguins.

The biggest draw being the cheeky seals with their interesting individual personalities they put on quite the show.

28. SEE 120 000 YEAR OLD FOOTPRINTS AND A COELACANTH

East London Museum has may marvels on display like the world's oldest footprints so far discovered.

A fish from a species that was believed to have gone extinct over 70-million years ago with weird limb-like-fins and a tail similar to that of a dog!

There are always travelling exhibits on display and a tea room offering decadent cakes and light meals.

29. BIG GAME FISHING IN THE WARM INDIAN OCEAN

If you want to go deep sea fishing in East London there are charters that can be hired from the East London boat club.

Leaving early in the morning you set off on the Indian Ocean in pursuit of deep sea fish, in season game fish and a shark or two.

The charters usually can take up to eightr people and supply all the equipment and bait.

The trips are normally up to eight hours and are weather dependant.

30. WHALE WATCHING AND DOLPHIN SPOTTING

Taking a stroll along Nahoon Beach Boardwalk after having a tasty lunch at the Reef Café is a great lazy Sunday Afternoon activity.

Take in the kilometers of unspoiled coastline and bird life while having a leisurely stroll.

Depending on the time of day one is sure to spot Dolphins catching a few waves.

In season it is a good view point from which to spot the Southern Right and Humpback whales that pass close by the shore line.

Even some Killer Whales have passed by from time to time.

31. SIGHT SEE FROM UP ABOVE

For a breathtaking different view of the Eastern Cape Coast line there are helicopter charters.

Fly above the busy roads and beaches taking in the sights from above for amazing photographs.

Get to see a bit of the rugged Wild Coast in a thrilling helicopter ride.

"I never knew of a morning in Africa when I woke up and was not happy"

– Ernest Hemingway

32. ROCK CLIMBING AND ABSEILING

For some thrilling rock climbs Morgan's bay just outside of East London has the largest sea cliff climbing area in South Africa.

Climbing can be done all year round and there are six hundred and twelve climbing routes.

There are some indoor climbing gyms in and around the Eastern Cape.

33. WATER SPORTS FOR EVERYONE

With endless sandy beaches to choose from East London has a vast array of water sports to choose from.

Surfing and Paddle Skiing being some of the main sports the town is known for having a lot of good spots for both sports and the friendly residents are always happy to point you in the direction of the action.

Boogie boarding in the ocean, canoeing along one of the many estuaries or for the more adventurous kayaking out on the ocean!

>TOURIST

34. A LAZY DAY WITH SURF, SEA AND SAND

Gonubie beaches have rock pools, great fishing and surfing spots.

On the Gonubie main beach you are bound to find at beach volley ball, touch rugby or beach cricket game to join.

Jump over or body surf in the waves or swim, splash and play in the winding river.

Watch the ski-boats launch from the river mouth and in season there is usually all sorts of events and water fun.

The beach is always buzzing with activity and families enjoying a good family day out.

35. BREAKFAST, LUNCH AND SUPPER WITH A VIEW

For a breakfast before you hit the beach Shelley's along the beach front in Gonubie offers a good breakfast whilst sitting out upon a deck and taking in the beautiful sea and main beach.

Pancakes are always delicious no matter the time of day the Heavenly Pancake House Restaurant in Gonubie offers a good selection of both savory and sweet with the added bonus of great views.

Sea food is an excellent way to round of the day and the Deck at the Gonubie Hotel offers a good Al la carte menu also overlooking the Gonubie Bay gently lapping the rocks and bathed in silver from the glow of the moon.

36. RELAX, UNWIND AND ENJOY GOOD COMPANY

At the end of an active sun filled day on the beach there is no better way to end it than with a sundowner at the local Gonubie Hotel.

With three bars to choose from each with a view of the sea and full of friendly locals always eager to make new friends there is no better way to unwind and cool down after a day baking in the sun!

On a Friday, Saturday and sometimes Sundays there is live music to tap your feet to and enjoy.

There would be no better way to explain an experience at the Gonubie Hotel than by the words of the theme song to the sitcom Cheers – "Where everybody knows your name"!

37. STEAK NIGHT AT THE SKI BOAT CLUB

Every month the Ski boat club on the banks of the Gonubie River has a steak night.

Big juicy steaks are grilled on an open fire; usually there is live music and or a sports game being aired on one of the many flat screens in the small club.

The sandy river banks a lit by flood lights and the kids partake in various activities on the sand.

There is a natural order in the Eastern Cape that the older kids look out for and take care of the younger ones as they all mix and mingle together partaking in various activities.

38. JUMP, AIM AND FIRE

You can jump to your hearts delight at Gravity Trampoline center at the Beacon Bay Crossing in East London.

Challenge someone to a game of Extreme Mini Golf.

Laser Tag is fun and you get to play up to three different laser tag courses depending on how long you have.

If you are a mom with younger ones and just want a coffee and to mingle with other like parents then Bubble Junction has a coffee shop where you can sit and watch your kid play in ball pits, jungle gyms and on soft blocks.

39. SHOPPING, SHOWS, FUN AND FAIR

Hemmingway's offers a bit of everything from a hotel with a casino and movie houses to many retail outlets and supermarkets.

The food court has many different cuisines to choose from most of which cater for kids with a form of play room.

The games center has formulae one type go-carting, bumper cars, ten pin bowling and arcade games.

Being a mom myself a trip to Hemmingway's is a shopping trip, with a lunch pit stop and an hour or so at the games center as a treat for the kids.

40. LIONS, CHEETAHS AND MORE

The Lion Park in East London is a wonderful day out for both the kids and adults alike.

There are lions, leopards and Cheetahs of which you can pre book a Cheetah experience.

Usually when there are lion cubs you are able to play with them, although they still do bite but there is nothing like the feeling of holding one.

The Giant turtles are a sight to see, although they do not do much they will attempt to amble over when you have feed in hand.

The tea room offers some great food and you can watch the animals and fend your food from the rabbits and friendly buck that wonder around inviting themselves to your tea.

There are usually various animal interactions at the park they do cost extra but are well worth it.

41. SNAKES ALIVE AND VENOM PITS

Python Park is a good educational centre that has snake interactions, must admit I have been to the park many times but personally keep a good distance from the snakes.

They have a big selection of snakes and even for one such as me it is truly fascinating to learn about the creatures.

The Venom Pit is one of the largest snake parks in Africa and they have some of the most deadly snakes in Africa as well as some of the rarest snakes.

If nothing else one comes away from there a bit more able to identify the difference between a venomous and non-venomous snake!

"Travel makes one modest, you see what a tiny place you occupy in the world"

– Gustave Flaubert

>TOURIST

42. CAMP IN THE BUSH ARENA

Just outside of East London The Arena Riverside Resort a camping and caravan park is frequented by locals and visitors all year round.

With a great restaurant, Spa and hair salon, camping and caravan facilities right along the river as well as self catering cottages to rent it caters for everyone.

Lots of action adventures like zip lining, canoeing down the river and in season planned events it is a great way to reconnect with family and nature.

Don't be surprised to find Abby the giraffe stopping by for a visit or to join in the fun. He also loves to kiss and cuddle – a legendary trade mark of his! He roams freely through the park with his herd of female giraffe friends.

43. HAVE YOU HUGGED AN ELEPHANT?

About ten kilometers or so outside East London is the Inkwenkwezi Private Game Reserve.

As with all the game parks in the Eastern Cape it is a malaria free zone.

The reserve has all the big five game which you get a chance to spot on one of the many daily guided game drives.

Although quite frightening it is quite something to get to park in the lion enclosure right next to the lions and lionesses basking in the sun.

My favorite time in this park is the interaction with African Elephants where you get to hold their trunks whilst you feed them, hug them as they wonder around you following your guide.

The lodge has really great food, Sunday roasts and on a Wednesday night they have a burger night with their legendary gigantic burgers.

44. TEA IN THE TREES ANYONE?

Not exactly on the Sunshine Coastal Route but just outside of East London in a small sea side village called Chintsa West is a restaurant set in a coastal forest setting.

The log style table and benches are set outside amongst the trees with a unique, healthy menu on offer.

It is only open on a Saturday and Sunday but well worth a drive with a market every first and last Sunday of the month.

45. PLACES TO STAY

There are many hotels along the Sunshine Coast each with lots of activities and facilities to offer. .

Staying in a hotel is always great but the Easten Cape is known for its friendly warmth and old worldly charm.

The best way to travel like a local is to stay at the many cozy Bed and Breakfasts dotted along the way.

These establishments make you feel like you have come home as you become part of their extended family!

46. FREE RANGE CHILDREN

There are many rural villages along the route where children run and play so it is crucial to stick to speed limits and adhere to the road signs warning of people crossing.

In the Eastern Cape the kids run around mostly barefoot and fancy free favoring the outdoors to being cooped inside.

There playful exuberance is very catchy and even the hardiest of indoor lovers soon becomes coaxed into joining the barefoot outdoor fun.

Most places you will visit be it a pub or adventure facility will cater for the younger generation.

It is an unwritten rule amongst the kids in any group that the eldest and more experienced of them takes care of and looks out for the younger ones.

47. POT HOLES FOR AFRICA

The one really frustrating thing about the Eastern Cape is the state of some of its roads.

So watch out for the pot holes in the road especially after a good rain fall as the size and depth of the hole can be a bit deceptive.

Always ensure there is a spare wheel in the vehicle you are driving and that it is has air in it.

It is advisable to get a portable air pump for peace of mind.

If renting a car ensure there is good roadside cover and that it operates in most of the major areas along the route of your trip.

48. SAFETY TIPS

In the major cities always keep your doors locked and windows rolled up.

Don't leave valuables or items of interest on the seats and rather place handbags, briefcases, camera cases, etc. in the boot.

Never stop for strangers no matter if it is a child standing on the road. Rather get the local police department to go attend to the person.

Always ensure bags are closed and hold onto them securely especially in the towns and shopping centers.

Always lock your valuables away when leaving your rooms or holiday accommodation.

49. CHECK THE LOCAL EVENTS

The cities and small sea-side towns have events all year round.

Not only are these events fun and usually incorporate something for the whole family to partake in but they are a great way to mingle and meet the friendly locals.

So always check out the "what's happening" in and around the towns and the planned events calendars for the place you are visiting.

50. WHAT TO WEAR WHEN YOU GET THERE

One of the things my friends from over-seas and even the Western Cape ask me is "What clothing must I bring?"

>TOURIST

We are basically a smart casual leaning more towards the casual dressers.

The night owls that seek out the vibrant night life tend to go for all the basic trending fashions.

There are some restaurants and functions you may be attending that require a bit more formal attire.

But mostly a t-shirt, jeans, sneakers or baggies (board shorts), t-shirt and flip-flops are the every-day choice.

The days are usually really warm but the nights can get a bit chilly so always have a jumper handy.

And I cannot stress this enough if out in the sun wear sun block and a hat!

>TOURIST

50 THINGS TO KNOW ABOUT PACKING LIGHT FOR TRAVEL

Pack the Right Way Every Time

Author: Manidipa Bhattacharyya

First Published in 2015 by Dr. Lisa Rusczyk. Copyright 2015. All Rights Reserved. No part of this publication may be reproduced, including scanning and photocopying, or distributed in any form or by any means, electronic or mechanical, or stored in a database or retrieval system without prior written permission from the publisher.

Disclaimer: The publisher has put forth an effort in preparing and arranging this book. The information provided herein by the author is provided "as is". Use this information at your own risk. The publisher is not a licensed doctor. Consult your doctor before engaging in any medical activities. The publisher and author disclaim any liabilities for any loss of profit or commercial or personal damages resulting from the information contained in this book.

Edited by Melanie Howthorne

ABOUT THE AUTHOR

Manidipa Bhattacharyya is a creative writer and editor, with an education in English literature and Linguistics. After working in the IT industry for seven long years she decided to call it quits and follow her heart instead. Manidipa has been ghost writing, editing, proof reading and doing secondary research services for many story tellers and article writers for about three years. She stays in Kolkata, India with her husband and a busy two year old. In her own time Manidipa enjoys travelling, photography and writing flash fiction.

Manidipa believes in travelling light and never carries anything that she couldn't haul herself on a trip. However, travelling with her child changed the scenario. She seemed to carry the entire world with her for the baby on the first two trips. But good sense prevailed and she is again working her way to becoming a light traveler, this time with a kid.

>TOURIST

He who would travel happily must travel light.

-Antoine de Saint-Exupéry

Travel takes you to different places from seas and mountains to deserts and much more. In your travels you get to interact with different people and their cultures. You will, however, enjoy the sights and interact positively with these new people even more, if you are travelling light.

When you travel light your mind can be free from worry about your belongings. You do not have to spend precious vacation time waiting for your luggage to arrive after a long flight. There is be no chance of your bags going missing and the best part is that you need not pay a fee for checked baggage.

People who have mastered this art of packing light will root for you to take only one carry-on, wherever you go. However, many people can find it really hard to pack light. More so if you are travelling with children. Differentiating between "must have" and "just in case" items is the starting point. There will be ample shopping avenues at your destination which are just waiting to be explored.

This book will show you 'packing' in a new 'light' – pun intended – and help you to embrace light packing practices for all of your future travels.

Off to packing!

DEDICATION

I dedicate this book to all the travel buffs that I know, who have given me great insights into the contents of their backpacks.

THE RIGHT TRAVEL GEAR

1. CHOOSE YOUR TRAVEL GEAR CAREFULLY

While selecting your travel gear, pick items that are light weight, durable and most importantly, easy to carry. There are cases with wheels so you can drag them along – these are usually on the heavy side because of the trolley. Alternatively a backpack that you can carry comfortably on your back, or even a duffel bag that you can carry easily by hand or sling across your body are also great options. Whatever you choose, one thing to keep in mind is that the luggage itself should not weigh a ton, this will give you the flexibility to bring along one extra pair of shoes if you so desire.

2. CARRY THE MINIMUM NUMBER OF BAGS

Selecting light weight luggage is not everything. You need to restrict the number of bags you carry as well. One carry-on size bag is ideal for light travel. Most carriers allow one cabin baggage plus one purse, handbag or camera bag as long as it slides under the seat in front. So technically, you can carry two items of luggage without checking them in.

3. PACK ONE EXTRA BAG

Always pack one extra empty bag along with your essential items. This could be a very light weight duffel bag or even a sturdy tote bag which takes up minimal space. In the event that you end up buying a lot of souvenirs, you already have a handy bag to stuff all that into and do not have to spend time hunting for an appropriate bag.

>TOURIST

I'm very strict with my packing and have everything in its right place. I never change a rule. I hardly use anything in the hotel room. I wheel my own wardrobe in and that's it.

Charlie Watts

CLOTHES & ACCESSORIES

4. PLAN AHEAD

Figure out in advance what you plan to do on your trip. That will help you to pick that one dress you need for the occasion. If you are going to attend a wedding then you have to carry formal wear. If not, you can ditch the gown for something lighter that will be comfortable during long walks or on the beach.

5. WEAR THAT JACKET

Remember that wearing items will not add extra luggage for your air travel. So wear that bulky jacket that you plan to carry for your trip. This saves space and can also help keep you warm during the chilly flight.

6. MIX AND MATCH

Carry clothes that can be interchangeably used to reinvent your look. Find one top that goes well with a couple of pairs of pants or skirts. Use tops, shirts and jackets wisely along with other accessories like a scarf or a stole to create a new look.

7. CHOOSE YOUR FABRIC WISELY

Stuffing clothes in cramped bags definitely takes its toll which results in wrinkles. It is best to carry wrinkle free, synthetic clothes or merino tops. This will eliminate the need for that small iron you usually bring along.

8. DITCH CLOTHES PACK UNDERWEAR

Pack more underwear and socks. These are the things that will give you a fresh feel even if you do not get a chance to wear fresh clothes. Moreover these are easy to wash and can be dried inside the hotel room itself.

9. CHOOSE DARK OVER LIGHT

While picking your clothes choose dark coloured ones. They are easy to colour coordinate and can last longer before needing a wash. Accidental food spills and dirt from the road are less visible on darker clothes.

10. WEAR YOUR JEANS

Take only one pair of Jeans with you, which you should wear on the flight. Remember to pick a pair that can be worn for sightseeing trips and is equally eloquent for dinner. You can add variety by adding light weight cargoes and chinos.

11. CARRY SMART ACCESSORIES

The right accessory can give you a fresh look even with the same old dress. An intelligent neck-piece, a couple of bright scarves, stoles or a sarong can be used in a number of ways to add variety to your clothing. These light weight beauties can double up as a nursing cover, a light blanket, beach wear, a modesty cover for visiting places of worship, and also makes for an enthralling game of peek-a-boo.

12. LEARN TO FOLD YOUR GARMENTS

Seasoned travellers all swear by rolling their clothes for compact and wrinkle free packing. Bundle packing, where you roll the clothes around a central object as if tying it up, is also a popular method of compact and wrinkle free packing. Stacking folded clothes one on top of another is a big no-no as it makes creases extreme and they are difficult to get rid of without ironing.

13. WASH YOUR DIRTY LAUNDRY

One of the ways to avoid carrying loads of clothes is to wash the clothes you carry. At some places you might get to use the laundry services or a Laundromat but if you are in a pinch, best solution is to wash them yourself. If that is the plan then carrying quick drying clothes is highly recommended, which most often also happen to be the wrinkle free variety.

14. LEAVE THOSE TOWELS BEHIND

Regular towels take up a lot of space, are heavy and take ages to dry out. If you are staying at hotels they will provide you with towels anyway. If you are travelling to a remote place, where the availability of towels look doubtful, carry a light weight travel towel of viscose material to do the job.

15. USE A COMPRESSION BAG

Compression bags are getting lots of recommendation now days from regular travellers. These are useful for saving space in your luggage when you have to pack bulky dresses. While packing for the return trip, get help from the hotel staff to arrange a vacuum cleaner.

FOOTWEAR

16. PUT ON YOUR HIKING BOOTS

If you have plans to go hiking or trekking during your trip, you will need those bulky hiking boots. The best way to carry them is to wear them on flight to save space and luggage weight. You can remove the boots once inside and be comfortable in your socks.

17. PICKING THE RIGHT SHOES

Shoes are often the bulkiest items, along with being the dainty if you are a female. They need care and take up a lot of space in your luggage. It is advisable therefore to pick shoes very carefully. If you plan to do a lot of walking and site seeing, then wearing a pair of comfortable walking shoes are a must. For more formal occasions you can carry durable, light weight flats which will not take up much space.

18. STUFF SHOES

If you happen to pack a pair of shoes, ensure you utilize their hollow insides. Tuck small items like rolled up socks or belts to save space. They will also be easy to find.

TOILETRIES

19. STASHING TOILETRIES

Carry only absolute necessities. Airline rules dictate that for one carry-on bag, liquids and gels must be in 3.4 ounce (100ml) bottles or less, and must be packed in a one quart zip-lock bag. If you are planning to stay in a hotel, the basic things will be provided for you. It's best is to buy the rest from the local market at your destination.

20. TAKE ALONG TAMPONS

Tampons are a hard to find item in a lot of countries. Figure out how many you need and pack accordingly. For longer stays you can buy them online and have them delivered to where you are staying.

21. GET PAMPERED BEFORE YOU TRAVEL

Some avid travellers suggest getting a pedicure and manicure just the day before travelling. This not only gives you a well kept look, you also save the trouble of packing nail polish. Remember, every little bit of weight reduced adds up.

ELECTRONICS

22. LUGGING ALONG ELECTRONICS

Electronics have a large role to play in our lives today. Most of us cannot imagine our lives away from our phones, laptops or tablets. However while travelling, one must consider the amount of weight these electronics add to our luggage. Thankfully smart phones come along with all the essentials tools like a camera, email access, picture editing tools and more. They are smart to the point of eliminating the need to carry multiple gadgets. Choose a smart phone that suits all your requirements and travel with the world in your palms or pocket.

23. REDUCE THE NUMBER OF CHARGERS

If you do travel with multiple electronic devices, you will have to bear the additional burden of carrying all their chargers too. Check if a single charger can be used for multiple devices. You might also consider investing in a pocket charger. These small devices support multiple devices while keeping you charged on the go.

24. TRAVEL FRIENDLY APPS

Along with smart phones come numerous apps, which are immensely helpful in our travels. You name it and you have an app for it at hand – take pictures, sharing with friends and family, torch to light dark roads, maps, checking flight/train times, find hotels and many other things. Use these smart alternatives to traditional items like books to eliminate weight and save space.

I get ideas about what's essential when packing my suitcase.

-Diane von Furstenberg

TRAVELLING WITH KIDS

25. BRING ALONG THE STROLLER

Kids might enjoy walking for a while but they soon tire out and a stroller is the just the right thing for them to rest in while you continue your tour. Strollers also double duty as a luggage carrier and shopping bag holder. Remember to pick a light weight, easy to handle brand of stroller. Better yet, find out in advance if you can rent a stroller at your destination.

26. BRING ONLY ENOUGH DIAPERS FOR YOUR TRIP

Diapers take up a lot of space and add to the weight of your luggage. Therefore it is advisable to carry just enough diapers to last through the trip and a few for afterwards, till you buy fresh stock at your destination. Unless of course you are travelling to a really remote area, in which case you have no choice but to carry the load. Otherwise diapers are something you will find pretty easily.

27. TAKE ONLY A COUPLE OF TOYS

Children are easily attracted by new things in their environment. While travelling they will find numerous 'new' objects to scrutinize and play with. Packing just one favorite toy is enough, or if there is no favorite toy leave out all of them in favor of stories or imaginary games.

28. CARRY KID FRIENDLY SNACKS

Create a small snack counter in your bag to store away quick bites for those sudden hunger pangs. Depending on the child's age this could include chocolates, raisins, dry fruits, granola bars or biscuits. Also keep a bottle of water handy for your little one. These things do not add much weight and can be adjusted in a handbag or knapsack.

29. GAMES TO CARRY

Create some travel specific, imaginary games if you have slightly grown up children, like spot the attractions. Keep a coloring book and colors handy for in-flight or hotel time. Apps on your smart phone can keep the children engaged with cartoons and story books. Older children are often entertained by games available on phones or tablets. This cuts the weight of luggage down while keeping the kids entertained.

30. LET THE KIDS CARRY THEIR LOAD

A good thing is to start early sharing of responsibilities. Let your child pick a bag of his or her choice and pack it themselves. Keep tabs on what they are stuffing in their bags by asking if they will be using that item on the trip. It could start out being just an entertainment bag initially but with growing years they will learn to sort the useful from the superfluous. Children as little as four can maneuver a small trolley suitcase like a pro- their experience in pull along toys credit. If you are worried that you may be pulling it for them, you may want to start with a backpack.

31. DECIDE ON LOCATION FOR CHILDREN TO SLEEP

While on a trip you might not always get a crib at your destination, and carrying one will make life all the more difficult. Instead call ahead to see if there are any cribs or roll out beds for children. You may even put blankets on the floor. Weave them a story about camping and they will gladly sleep without any trouble.

32. GET BABY PRODUCTS DELIVERED AT YOUR DESTINATION

If you are absolutely paranoid about not getting your favourite variety of diaper or brand of baby food, check out online stores like amazon.com for services in your destination city. You can buy things online ahead of your travel and get them delivered to your hotel upon arrival.

33. FEEDING NEEDS OF YOUR INFANTS

If you are travelling with a breastfed infant, you save the trouble of carrying bottles and bottle sanitization kits. For special food, or medications, you may need to call ahead to make sure you have a refrigerator where you are staying.

34. FEEDING NEEDS OF YOUR TODDLER

With the progression from infancy to toddler, their dietary requirements too evolve. You will have to pack some snacks for travelling time. Fresh fruits and vegetables can be purchased at your destination. Most of the cities you travel to in whichever part of the world, will have baby food products and formulas, available at the local drug-store or the supermarket.

35. PICKING CLOTHES FOR YOUR BABY

Contrary to popular belief, babies can do without many changes of clothes. At the most pack 2 outfits per day. Pack mix and match type clothes for your little one as well. Pick things which are comfortable to wear and quick to dry.

36. SELECTING SHOES FOR YOUR BABY

Like outfits, kids can make do with two pairs of comfortable shoes. If you can get some water resistant shoes it will be best. To expedite drying wet shoes, you can stuff newspaper in them then wrap them with newspaper and leave them to dry overnight.

37. KEEP ONE CHANGE OF CLOTHES HANDY

Travelling with kids can be tricky. Keep a change of clothes for the kids and mum handy in your purse or tote bag. This takes a bit of space in your hand luggage but comes extremely handy in case there are any accidents or spills.

38. LEAVE BEHIND BABY ACCESSORIES

Baby accessories like their bed, bath tub, car seat, crib etc. should be left at home. Many hotels provide a crib on request, while car seats can be borrowed from friends or rented. Babies can be given a bath in the hotel sink or even in the adult bath tub with a little bit of water. If you bring a few bath toys, they can be used in the bath, pool, and out of water. They can also be sanitized easily in the sink.

39. CARRY A SMALL LOAD OF PLASTIC BAGS

With children around there are chances of a number of soiled clothes and diapers. These plastic bags help to sort the dirt from the clean inside your big bag. These are very light weight and come in handy to other carry stuff as well at times.

PACK WITH A PURPOSE

40. PACKING FOR BUSINESS TRIPS

One neutral-colored suit should suffice. It can be paired with different shirts, ties and accessories for different occasions. One pair of black suit pants could be worn with a matching jacket for the office or with a snazzy top for dinner.

41. PACKING FOR A CRUISE

Most cruises have formal dinners, and that formal dress usually takes up a lot of space. However you might find a tuxedo to rent. For women, a short black dress with multiple accessory options will do the trick.

42. PACKING FOR A LONG TRIP OVER DIFFERENT CLIMATES

The secret packing mantra for travel over multiple climates is layering. Layering traps air around your body creating insulation against the cold. The same light t-shirt that is comfortable in a warmer climate can be the innermost layer in a colder climate.

REDUCE SOME MORE WEIGHT

43. LEAVE PRECIOUS THINGS AT HOME

Things that you would hate to lose or get damaged leave them at home. Precious jewelry, expensive gadgets or dresses, could be anything. You will not require these on your trip. Leave them at home and spare the load on your mind.

44. SEND SOUVENIRS BY MAIL

If you have spent all your money on purchasing souvenirs, carrying them back in the same bag that you brought along would be difficult. Either pack everything in another bag and check it in the airport or get everything shipped to your home. Use an international carrier for a secure transit, but this could be more expensive than the checking fees at the airport.

45. AVOID CARRYING BOOKS

Books equal to weight. There are many reading apps which you can download on your smart phone or tab. Plus there are gadgets like Kindle and Nook that are thinner and lighter alternatives to your regular book.

CHECK, GET, SET, CHECK AGAIN

46. STRATEGIZE BEFORE PACKING

Create a travel list and prepare all that you think you need to carry along. Keep everything on your bed or floor before packing and then think through once again – do I really need that? Any item that meets this question can be avoided. Remove whatever you don't really need and pack the rest.

47. TEST YOUR LUGGAGE

Once you have fully packed for the trip take a test trip with your luggage. Take your bags and go to town for window shopping for an hour. If you enjoy your hour long trip it is good to go, if not, go home and reduce the load some more. Repeat this test till you hit the right weight.

48. ADD A ROLL OF DUCT TAPE

You might wonder why, when this book has been talking about reducing stuff, we're suddenly asking you to pack something totally unusual. This is because when you have limited supplies, duct tape is immensely helpful for small repairs – a broken bag, leaking zip-lock bag, broken sunglasses, you name it and duct tape can fix it, temporarily.

49. LIST OF ESSENTIAL ITEMS

Even though the emphasis is on packing light, there are things which have to be carried for any trip. Here is our list of essentials:

- Passport/Visa or any other ID
- Any other paper work that might be required on a trip like permits, hotel reservation confirmations etc.
- Medicines – all your prescription medicines and emergency kit, especially if you are travelling with children
- Medical or vaccination records
- Money in foreign currency if travelling to a different country
- Tickets- Email or Message them to your phone

>TOURIST

50. MAKE THE MOST OF YOUR TRIP

Wherever you are going, whatever you hope to do we encourage you to embrace it whole-heartedly. Take in the scenery, the culture and above all, enjoy your time away from home.

On a long journey even a straw weighs heavy.

-Spanish Proverb

>TOURIST

PACKING AND PLANNING TIPS

A Week before Leaving

- Arrange for someone to take care of pets and water plants.
- Stop mail and newspaper.
- Notify Credit Card companies where you are going.
- Change your thermostat settings.
- Car inspected, oil is changed, and tires have the correct pressure.
- Passports and photo identification is up to date.
- Pay bills.
- Copy important items and download travel Apps.
- Start collecting small bills for tips.

Right Before Leaving

- Clean out refrigerator.
- Empty garbage cans.
- Lock windows.
- Make sure you have the proper identification with you.
- Bring cash for tips.
- Remember travel documents.
- Lock door behind you.
- Remember wallet.
- Unplug items in house and pack chargers.

>TOURIST

- ## GREATER THAN A TOURIST SERIES BOOKS

  •

Greater Than a Tourist: Australia: 250 Travel Tips from Locals

Greater Than a Tourist-Caribbean: 500 Travel Tips from Locals

Greater Than a Tourist – China : 300 Travel Tips from Locals

Greater Than a Tourist- India: 500 Travel Tips from Locals

Greater Than a Tourist-Kenya: 300 Travel Tips from Locals

Greater Than a Tourist - ITALY: 400 Travel Tips from Locals

Greater than a Tourist- Pakistan: 250 Travel Tips from a Locals

Greater Than a Tourist- Romania: 250 Travel Tips from Locals

Greater Than a Tourist- Serbia: 250 Travel Tips from a Locals

Greater Than a Tourist- Spain: 350 Travel Tips from Locals

Greater Than a Tourist- South Africa: 300 Travel Tips from Locals

READ OTHER GREATER THAN A TOURIST BOOKS

Greater Than a Tourist San Miguel de Allende Guanajuato Mexico: 50 Travel Tips from a Local by Tom Peterson

Greater Than a Tourist – Lake George Area New York USA: 50 Travel Tips from a Local by Janine Hirschklau

Greater Than a Tourist – Monterey California United States: 50 Travel Tips from a Local by Katie Begley

Greater Than a Tourist – Chanai Crete Greece: 50 Travel Tips from a Local by Dimitra Papagrigoraki

Greater Than a Tourist – The Garden Route Western Cape Province South Africa: 50 Travel Tips from a Local by Li-Anne McGregor van Aardt

Greater Than a Tourist – Sevilla Andalusia Spain: 50 Travel Tips from a Local by Gabi Gazon

Greater Than a Tourist – Kota Bharu Kelantan Malaysia: 50 Travel Tips from a Local by Aditi Shukla

Children's Book: Charlie the Cavalier Travels the World by Lisa Rusczyk

> TOURIST

Visit Greater Than a Tourist for Free Travel Tips
   http://GreaterThanATourist.com

Sign up for the Greater Than a Tourist Newsletter for discount days, new books, and travel information: http://eepurl.com/cxspyf

Follow us on Facebook for tips, images, and ideas:
   https://www.facebook.com/GreaterThanATourist

Follow us on Pinterest for travel tips and ideas:
   http://pinterest.com/GreaterThanATourist

Follow us on Instagram for beautiful travel images:
   http://Instagram.com/GreaterThanATourist

> TOURIST

At Greater Than a Tourist, we love to share travel tips with you. How did we do? What guidance do you have for how we can give you better advice for your next trip? Please send your feedback to GreaterThanaTourist@gmail.com as we continue to improve the series. We appreciate your constructive feedback. Thank you.

>TOURIST

METRIC CONVERSIONS

TEMPERATURE

110° F — — 40° C
100° F —
90° F — — 30° C
80° F —
70° F — — 20° C
60° F —
50° F — — 10° C
40° F —
32° F — — 0° C
20° F —
10° F — — -10° C
0° F —
-10° F — — -18° C
-20° F — — -30° C

To convert F to C:
Subtract 32, and then multiply by 5/9 or .5555.

To Convert C to F:
Multiply by 1.8 and then add 32.

32F = 0C

LIQUID VOLUME

To Convert:...............Multiply by
U.S. Gallons to Liters............... 3.8
U.S. Liters to Gallons 26
Imperial Gallons to U.S. Gallons 1.2
Imperial Gallons to Liters........ 4.55
Liters to Imperial Gallons 22
**1 Liter = .26 U.S. Gallon
1 U.S. Gallon = 3.8 Liters**

DISTANCE

To convert ....Multiply by
Inches to Centimeters 2.54
Centimeters to Inches 39
Feet to Meters........................3
Meters to Feet 3.28
Yards to Meters 91
Meters to Yards 1.09
Miles to Kilometers 1.61
Kilometers to Miles............ .62
**1 Mile = 1.6 km
1 km = .62 Miles**

WEIGHT

1 Ounce = .28 Grams
1 Pound = .4555 Kilograms
1 Gram = .04 Ounce
1 Kilogram = 2.2 Pounds

TRAVEL QUESTIONS

- Do you bring presents home to family or friends after a vacation?
- Do you get motion sick?
- Do you have a favorite billboard?
- Do you know what to do if there is a flat tire?
- Do you like a sun roof open?
- Do you like to eat in the car?
- Do you like to wear sun glasses in the car?
- Do you like toppings on your ice cream?
- Do you use public bathrooms?
- Did you bring your cell phone and does it have power?
- Do you have a form of identification with you?
- Have you ever been pulled over by a cop?
- Have you ever given money to a stranger on a road trip?
- Have you ever taken a road trip with animals?
- Have you ever went on a vacation alone?
- Have you ever run out of gas?
- If you could move to any place in the world, where would it be?
- If you could travel anywhere in the world, where would you travel?
- If you could travel in any vehicle, which one would it be?

>TOURIST

- If you had three things to wish for from a magic genie, what would they be?
- If you have a driver's license, how many times did it take you to pass the test?
- What are you the most afraid of on vacation?
- What do you want to get away from the most when you are on vacation?
- What foods smells bad to you?
- What item do you bring on ever trip with you away from home?
- What makes you sleepy?
- What song would you love to hear on the radio when you're cruising on the highway?
- What travel job would you want the least?
- What will you miss most while you are away from home?
- What is something you always wanted to try?
- What is the best road side attraction that you ever saw?
- What is the farthest distance you ever biked?
- What is the farthest distance you ever walked?
- What is the weirdest thing you needed to buy while on vacation?
- What is your favorite candy?
- What is your favorite color car?
- What is your favorite family vacation?
- What is your favorite food?
- What is your favorite gas station drink or food?
- What is your favorite license plate design?

- What is your favorite restaurant?
- What is your favorite smell?
- What is your favorite song?
- What is your favorite sound that nature makes?
- What is your favorite thing to bring home from a vacation?
- What is your favorite vacation with friends?
- What is your favorite way to relax?
- Where is the farthest place you ever traveled in a car?
- Where is the farthest place you ever went North, South, East and West?
- Where is your favorite place in the world?
- Who is your favorite singer?
- Who taught you how to drive?
- Who will you miss the most while you are away?
- Who if the first person you will contact when you get to your destination?
- Who brought you on your first vacation?
- Who likes to travel the most in your life?
- Would you rather be hot or cold?
- Would you rather drive above, below, or at the speed limited?
- Would you rather drive on a highway or a back road?
- Would you rather go on a train or a boat?
  - Would you rather go to the beach or the woods?

Printed in Great Britain
by Amazon